GREAT NEGROES

PAST AND PRESENT

VOLUME TWO

JAWANZA KUNJUFU
ERICA MYLES
NICHELLE WILSON

African American Images

Front cover illustration by Tony Quaid

First edition, first printing

ACKNOWLEDGMENT

We'd like to express our sincere appreciation

for the support of the

A.C. Bilbrew Library,

the Black Resource Center (Los Angeles),

and

the Chicago Woodson Regional Library's

Vivian Harsh Collection.

CONTENTS

INTRODUCTION

We at African American Images would like to thank all of you who made *Great Negroes Past and Present* a bestseller since its release in 1963. The book was the first of its kind. This was before the Black Power movement. We wanted to encourage, reconfirm, and teach Americans the rich legacy and contributions of African people.

At that time, Negro was the acceptable term. With the publication of this second volume, we had the same challenge as the NAACP, who also pondered changing the name to Black, Afro-American, African American, or African. They decided, as we did for a myriad of reasons, that the name should remain the same for legal, copyright, and consistency.

I was inspired to write this book because so many African American youth have asked me, "Do you have to die to be a famous African American?" It appeared that the only famous African Americans were dead. Volume Two is a collection of predominately contemporary African Americans who have made major contributions in their fields. Our editorial board felt the need for some of our great ancestors to also be included in this contemporary edition. One of the challenges involved in producing Volume Two is that the book is dated at the very first printing. With so many of our great people still alive while you're reading, they have written another book, made another film, won another election, discovered a cure for AIDS, sickle cell, and cancer, led another million person march, sang another platinum song, started another business, broke another sports record, improved the academic achievement of our children, married, divorced, and had children.

Another major challenge was the selection of the people. The editorial board of African American Images wanted a numerical balance in all fields. There is an unfortunate perception that Africans can rap better than they can read, are more accomplished in sports than in science, in music than math, and in basketball than biology. I wonder how many of you could name five living African Americans who are accomplished in math and science. That's why we have put science, technology, and health first and athletics and entertainment last. We value both but are concerned about the media that seem to promote our athletes and entertainers but not our engineers and doctors.

How do you choose 160 people out of 40 million? We could have easily filled the slots with African Americans in each sports Hall of Fame, the CEO's of Black Enterprise's top 100 businesses, or the highest ranking African Americans of Fortune 500 companies.

The list could have also been filled with the 8,000 plus elected officials or the pastors of all churches with a congregation greater than 3,000 members (as well as those who are anointed and doing great work with ten members in their living room). The book could have been filled with every African American who won a Grammy in the past decade.

Easily we could do a third volume of up and coming African Americans. There is a wealth of young talent in science, education, business, government, the arts, community activism, religion, athletics, and entertainment. A major criterion for this book was not just greatness, but consistency. Don't worry, Lauryn Hill, just keep doing your thing, and you will make Volume Three!

We hope you enjoy the book.

Jawanza Kunjufu

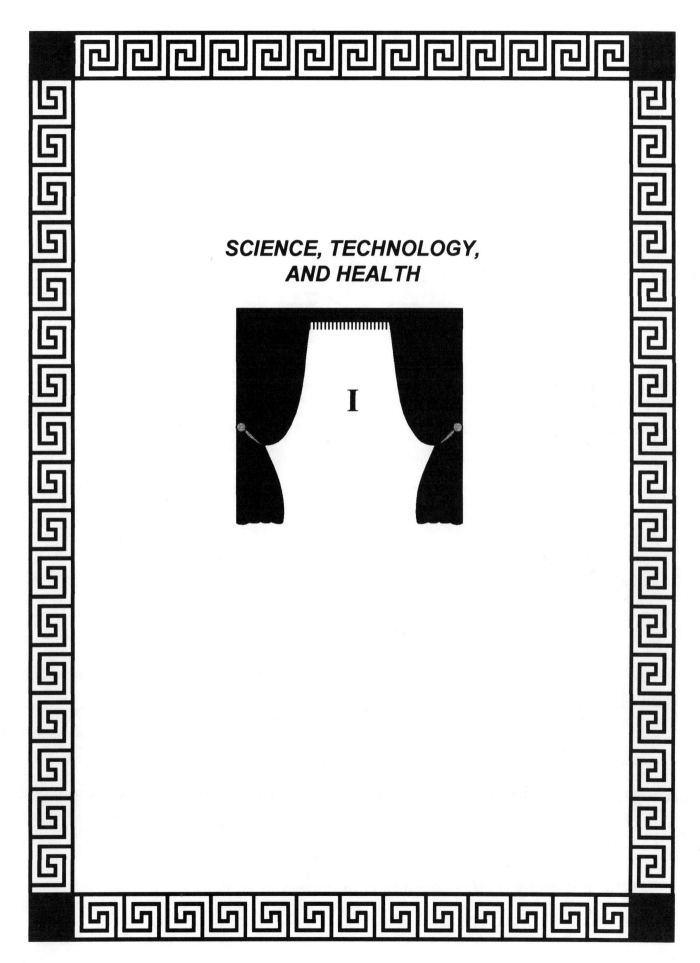

SCIENCE, TECHNOLOGY, AND HEALTH

I

Dr. Shirley Ann Jackson
(1946–)
PHYSICIST

Shirley Ann Jackson was born in Washington, D.C. She credits her love of science to her parents, especially her dad, who helped her to construct science projects. She graduated as valedictorian of Roosevelt High School in 1964. She entered the Massachusetts Institute of Technology and earned a bachelor's degree in Physics in 1968. Jackson became the first African American woman to earn a Ph.D. from MIT in 1973. Her research was in theoretical elementary particle physics and was directed by James Young, the first full-time tenured Black professor in the Physics department.

Jackson has made major theoretical contributions to physics, including research in the three-body scattering problem, charge density waves in layered compounds, polaronic aspects of electrons in the surface of liquid helium films, and the optical and electronic properties of semiconductor strained layer superlattices.

Jackson was a professor of physics at Rutgers from 1991–1995. She is the first African American chairperson of the United States Nuclear Regulatory Commission. She has been appointed to numerous boards, including the New Jersey Commission on Science and Technology, the National Academy of Sciences, the American Association for the Advancement of Science, and the National Science Foundation. In 1999, Jackson became the president of Renesselaer Polytechnic Institute in Troy, New York.

She has published more than 100 scientific articles and abstracts. Many appeared in *Annals of Physics, Physical Review, Applied Physics Letters,* and *Journal of Applied Physics.*

Jackson is married to a physicist and they have one son.

Dr. Ronald McNair
(1950–1986)
PHYSICIST AND ASTRONAUT

Ronald McNair was born in Lake City, South Carolina. Early on, his parents and teachers knew that there was something unique about McNair. He had a strong love of reading and a very inquisitive mind. He was valedictorian of his high school class. He enrolled at North Carolina A&T because of the school's emphasis on science. He graduated magna cum laude in physics.

McNair loved scholarship and continued on for his doctorate at the Massachusetts Institute of Technology. He earned a Ph.D. in physics at the young age of 26. He was a Presidential Scholar and Ford Foundation Distinguished National Scientist. He began working with the Hughes Research Corporation. McNair developed an expertise in laser physics.

McNair always had a desire to be an astronaut. Unfortunately, there had only been one African American to fly in space (Guy Bluford). McNair knew he was qualified and NASA agreed. McNair trained and prepared himself for several years. Finally, on June 28, 1986, he had his first opportunity on the Space Shuttle Challenger. Unfortunately, there were complications, and all seven crew members died. It was a major loss to the families, NASA, and the country.

The United States Department of Education established training, assistance, and scholarships for low-income students pursuing doctorates in engineering in the name of Ron McNair. Other organizations have created scholarships from other organizations in his name. Many science clubs nationwide are named in his honor.

Ron held a fifth degree belt in karate and was an accomplished jazz saxophonist. He is survived by a wife and two children.

Bessie Coleman
(1893–1926)
AVIATOR

Born in Texas in 1893, she was raised by a single mother from the time she was seven years old. A good student who excelled in math, Coleman briefly attended what is now Langston University in Oklahoma. She paid her way through school by taking in laundry. She left Langston after one semester for financial reasons and moved to Chicago to live with her brother. In Chicago, Coleman worked first as a manicurist and later as a restaurant manager near the Bridgeport neighborhood.

Coleman read everything she could get her hands on about current events. This began her interest in aviation, a field still in its infancy. Coleman decided to become an aviator. She set three goals for herself: first, to learn to fly and earn a pilot's license; second, to become a successful stunt pilot; and third, to start an aviation school so that young Blacks would not have to deal with racism in the field. Bessie Coleman's desire to take to the sky broke ground for Black people in many areas of aviation. Coleman was the first Black female pilot since the Wright brothers' first flew in 1903.

Learning to fly was not as easy as Coleman had expected. It was not that she had any great difficulty in mastering the skills and techniques. The problem was that the flight schools she had applied to were not willing to give a Black woman the opportunity. Her applications were rejected and Coleman became discouraged.

Chicago Defender newspaper founder Robert S. Abbott knew what it was like to face opposition to one's dreams. He did not want to see Coleman give up on her goals. He suggested an alternative to the racially exclusive American schools to which Coleman had applied. With Abbott's encouragement, Coleman learned to speak French and went overseas to study under some of Europe's finest pilots. Coleman returned to the United States in 1921 with her international pilot's license, finely tuned flying skills, and a new determination.

Her first goal accomplished, Coleman set out to use her new skills to make a name for herself as a popular exhibition flyer. In 1922, Coleman burst onto the U.S. scene in an air show sponsored by her friend Abbott. Several weeks later, she appeared in a show at what is now Midway Airport in Chicago. Coleman's daring techniques astounded the crowds and earned the petite, attractive pilot the nicknames "Brave Bessie" and "Queen Bess."

Just as Coleman's career began to soar, the young aviator met with tragedy. In April 1926, Coleman was preparing for a Memorial Day air show to benefit the Negro Welfare League in Jacksonville, Florida. Her equipment malfunctioned, and Coleman was thrown 500 feet from the plane to her death. Coleman died at the age of 33, doing exactly what she loved.

Coleman left her mark on the country and the world. Her body rests in Lincoln Cemetery. Today, Bessie Coleman Drive at O'Hare Airport in Chicago pays homage to the little woman whose big dreams took her beyond the clouds.

Lewis Latimer
(1848–1928)
INVENTOR

Lewis Latimer was born in suburban Boston. Later his father deserted the family when Lewis was very young. Lewis dropped out of school at the age of ten to help his mother and four siblings survive. He joined the Union Navy in 1864 and became a lieutenant in the fourth Battalion of the Massachusetts Militia.

After the Civil War, Latimer worked for a patent attorney as an office boy. There he learned drafting and electrical engineering. He used his meager wages to buy secondhand tools and constantly observed his employers. The firm Crosby and Gould promoted Latimer to chief draftsmen. One of his clients was Alexander Graham Bell. Latimer contributed to the design of the telephone.

Latimer was a highly sought after electrical engineer. Companies in the competitive incandescent lamp industry fought to hire Latimer. He worked for many of these companies, but in 1884 Thomas Edison hired him and paid him very well. The top scientists for the company were called Edison Pioneers and Latimer was a leading member of this distinguished group. The combination of his technical expertise and his experience with other companies made him a very valuable employee. Latimer kept Edison abreast of competitors' progress and was an expert witness in many court challenges about patents.

His book, *Incandescent Electric Lighting: A Practical Description of the Edison System* (1890) enhanced his status as an expert witness. Latimer also worked on his inventions and secured many patents for his many inventions, including a mechanism that enhanced railroad cars and cooling and disinfecting devices on train cars. He spent his retirement years as an independent consultant, teacher, musician, and poet.

Dr. Mae C. Jemison

(1956–)

ASTRONAUT AND PHYSICIAN

Mae Jemison knew early in life that she wanted to become an astronaut. Always an intelligent child, Jemison developed an interest in science with the encouragement of her uncle. This interest led her to become the first and only Black woman astronaut in the United States.

Born in Decatur, Alabama, Jemison was one of three children born to a maintenance worker and a schoolteacher. Her parents moved the family to Chicago to provide better educational opportunities for their children. In the school library, Jemison began to spend hours reading everything she could find on subjects like archaeology and anthropology. Those closest to Jemison recognized her enthusiasm for learning and encouraged her to find out more and more.

As a student at Morgan Park High School on Chicago's South Side, Jemison attended a field trip to a university in the area. This visit introduced her to the idea of choosing biomedical engineering as a profession. When she entered Stanford University in 1973, she switched her focus slightly and earned a bachelor's degree in chemical engineering. Because of her pride in her culture and her desire to learn more about her heritage, Jemison earned a second bachelor's degree in African American studies.

In 1977, Jemison entered medical school at Cornell University. It was during this time that her interest in science began to focus on the study of health within the international context. Jemison wanted to see firsthand how health issues were addressed in other countries. She spent one summer as a volunteer in a Cambodian refugee camp in Thailand. In 1979, she traveled to Kenya to study health issues. Jemison graduated from Cornell medical school in 1981, and in 1983 she served in West Africa as the area Peace Corps medical officer for Sierra Leone and Liberia.

Soon after Jemison returned to the United States, she learned that her application to NASA had been accepted. However, the January 1986 Space Challenger accident which claimed the lives of seven astronauts suspended NASA's astronaut selection process. The tragedy saddened Jemison, but it did not diminish her determination to become a space explorer.

Jemison reapplied and became one of only fifteen individuals selected from a pool of about two thousand. After a one-year training program, Mae C. Jemison became a mission specialist for NASA's space program in 1988. On September 12, 1992, when the space shuttle Endeavor lifted off, Jemison was aboard and became the first African American woman in space. In 1990, a monument to African American achievement in the skies was unveiled at Lambert-Saint Louis International Airport. The piece honors 75 African American aviation pioneers, including Jemison and Bessie Coleman, the first Black woman pilot. What started as a simple love of science has taken Jemison all over the country, all over the world, and even into outer space.

Dr. Guy Bluford
(1942–)
ASTRONAUT

Guy Bluford was born and raised in Philadelphia. His father was a mechanical engineer and loved going to work. Guy observed his dad and hoped that he could become an engineer. In high school, a counselor suggested that Guy was not college material. Guy and his parents paid no attention to him and he attended Penn State University.

Guy graduated with a bachelor's degree in engineering in 1964. He joined the U.S. Air Force and took flight training. Between 1964 and 1974, a metamorphosis took place within Bluford. He became more disciplined and focused. As a result, he ranked in the top 10 percent of his class. He received his master's degree (1974) and doctorate in aerospace engineering with a minor in laser graphics in 1978. He worked as a test pilot and an instructor for military aviators.

In 1978, Bluford submitted his application to the Space Shuttle program. He believed he had little chance with 8,000 people applying for only 35 openings. Surprisingly, Bluford was selected and he made the most of his opportunities. He was the first African American to reach outer space in 1983. Bluford has clocked more than 300 hours in space.

In 1993, he resigned from NASA to develop his own computer software company, in which he serves as vice-president. Bluford has received numerous awards and more than ten honorary doctor-ates. He is married and has two children.

Dr. George Carruthers
(1939–)
ASTROPHYSICIST

George Carruthers was born in Cincinnati, Ohio, and reared in Chicago by his parents. He was an excellent high school student. Carruthers earned a bachelor's degree in aerospace engineering from the University of Illinois. He earned his master's in physics and doctorate in astronautical engineering from the same school. From 1964 to 1982, Carruthers researched rocket astronomy and atomic nitrogen recombination in the Naval Research Laboratory. Carruthers is also an inventor.

From 1972 to 1973, Carruthers was the principal scientist responsible for developing a special camera that made the trip to the moon. It is called the far-ultraviolet camera/spectrograph. The 50-pound gold-plated unit was designed to study the earth's upper atmosphere and other interplanetary conditions. More than 200 frames and pictures were made of eleven selected targets. In 1973, another model of the camera was made and attached to Skylab 4 to take pictures of a comet speeding toward the sun.

In 1987, Carruthers was named Black Engineer of the Year. He is the editor of *National Technical Association Journal*. He is an active member of Project Smart, to encourage youth to pursue math and science.

Carruthers continues to work at the NASA Space Division in Mountain View, California, and consults for various laboratories.

Dr. Walter E. Massey

(1938–)

PHYSICIST AND EDUCATOR

Walter E. Massey was born in Hattiesburg, Mississippi. He cannot remember a time when he was not interested in math and related subjects. However, his primary and secondary education had not adequately prepared him for a career in math. He earned a bachelor's degree in physics from Morehouse in 1958.

Massey became interested in physics because of its relationship to math. Physics provided a useful way to apply math to understanding the physical world. Massey continued his education in the North. His undergraduate work in physics had assured him that he was on the right path to a satisfying career. He earned his doctorate in physics from Washington University in St. Louis in 1966. He left the Midwest and headed east to work as a professor and dean at Brown University in Rhode Island from 1971-1979. He founded Brown's Inner City Teachers of Science program. The organization trained teachers to teach science in urban schools. Massey also served as its first director.

In 1979, Massey became the director of Argonne National Laboratory. While there, he was an administrator at the University of Illinois at Chicago. In 1982, he became vice president at the University of Chicago.

In 1987, Walter Massey was elected president of the American Association for the Advancement of Science (AAAS). The AAAS is the largest–and one of the oldest and most respected–general science organizations in the country. The AAAS was first established in 1848. Massey's election marked the first time that the organization ever had an African American president.

Walter Massey returned to Morehouse, his alma mater, in 1995 as its 9th president. His vision is to prepare African American men for the twenty-first century which, of course, includes a strong foundation in math and science.

Despite his many responsibilities, Massey still finds time to lend his support to the advancement of science. He has served on two National Science Foundation committees and on the boards of the Museum of Science and Industry in Chicago, Brown University, and the American Association for the Advancement of Science.

He is married with two sons.

Dr. Marc Hannah

(1956–)

ENGINEER

Marc Regis Hannah was born and raised in Chicago, Illinois. He is the second youngest of five children, who were all inspired by their parents to value education. He earned his bachelor's degree from the Illinois Institute of Technology in electrical engineering and his master's and doctor's degrees from Stanford University.

While at Stanford, Hannah searched for a research project for his dissertation. He wanted something challenging, relevant, and enjoyable. One of his professors, Jim Clark, specialized in graphics. They spent hours together trying to develop a desktop computer system that would enable users to create realistic looking 3D images that could be shaded, and colored, moved, and manipulated interactively. Their vision became a reality, and Silicon Graphics SGI) was born in 1981. It is now a $3 billion company and employs approximately 11,000 people.

While Dr. Hannah served as chief scientist and later also as vice president of SGI, their computers created the special effects of movies such as *Terminator 2, The Abyss, The Hunt for Red October, Field of Dreams, Beauty and the Beast,* and *Lawnmower Man.* Silicon Graphics produced the visuals for the opening scenes of *Monday Night Football* and Michael Jackson's videos *Remember the Time* and *Black and White.* Hannah has worked with Nintendo and the video game Ultra 64. Silicon Graphics has also collaborated with Time Warner and Steven Spielberg's DreamWorks.

Hannah led the project to develop the Personal Iris workstation, the first of its kind below $20,000, and Indigo and Indy workstations which were priced below $5,000. Hannah is an investor and a board member of Silicon Magic, a company that supplies high-speed memory and media processing chips for personal computers. His consulting firm is Hannah Technologies. Hannah has been granted thirteen patents; others are pending.

Hannah serves on the Board of Overseers at Illinois Institute of Technology's (IIT) Institute of Design. He also served on the Board of Trustees at ITT. A room at his alma mater is named in his honor. In honor of his mother, Hannah created an ITT scholarship award for African American students. A science club in a high school in Oakland, California, is named in his honor. Hannah has received numerous awards and has been featured in major magazines and newspapers. He received the Black Engineer Award in 1988 for Outstanding Technical Contribution. He was one of 16 featured scientists in the exhibit, "Black Achievers in Science," which opened in 1987 at Chicago's Museum of Science and Industry and traveled to other museums throughout the country from 1988 through 1991.

Dr. Jocelyn Elders
(1933–)
DOCTOR

Jocelyn Elders was born in Schaal, Arkansas, the oldest of seven siblings. Her family was poor, and she walked thirteen miles to school. Elders loved to read and would be found near a kerosene lamp at night. She received a scholarship at age fifteen to Philander Smith College in Little Rock. She received a bachelor's degree in 1952.

Elders was amazed when Edith Irby Jones, the first African American to study medicine at the University of Arkansas, spoke at Philander. Jocelyn had never met an African American doctor. This was a turning point in Elders' life. She decided she wanted to become a doctor. She was accepted in the University of Arkansas and was the only African American woman with two Black males to attend. She graduated from medical school in 1960. She also earned a master's degree in biochemistry from the same university in 1971. She was a professor in pediatrics at the university from 1971 through 1976.

In 1977, she was named national advisor to the U.S. Food and Drug Administration. In 1987, Governor Bill Clinton named Elders director of the Arkansas Department of Health. Once again, this was the first time an African American had held that position. One of her many concerns was the cost of teen pregnancy to the state.

In 1993, President Clinton nominated Elders to serve as U.S. Surgeon General, and the Senate approved. Dr. Elders has always been outspoken about her beliefs. Some of her views were considered very drastic for the political arena. She favored pro-choice and the distribution of condoms. She chose masturbation over sexual intercourse outside of marriage. She recommended legalizing drugs to reduce crime and decrease profits. These views did not sit well with the conservative element of the country. President Clinton demanded her resignation in 1994. She did not regret her positions.

She returned to the University of Arkansas as a professor. Her major interest is the reduction of tobacco use among youth. She is a highly sought after speaker. She is married with two sons.

Dr. Benjamin Carson
(1951–)
NEUROSURGEON

Ben Carson was born in Detroit and has one brother. He was raised in poverty by a divorced mother. He was failing school and spent more time fighting than studying. His mother knew her sons were not working to their full potential. She devised a strategy that would greatly limit television and replaced it with reading books and writing reports. Initially, Ben resisted, but began to love traveling around the world, meeting new people, and learning new ideas through books. He fell in love with medicine and wanted to be a doctor.

His grades improved tremendously, and he won a scholarship to Yale University. He earned a bachelor's degree in 1973. He entered medical school at the University of Michigan and graduated in 1977 with the concentration in neurosurgery. He did his internship at the elite Johns Hopkins Hospital in Baltimore. He became the hospital's first-ever African American neurosurgical resident. He relocated to Western Australia because they had a shortage of neurosurgeons. This afforded him an opportunity to perform hundreds of surgeries.

He returned to Johns Hopkins in 1985 and became one of the hospital's leading surgeons. Within a year, he was promoted to director of pediatric neurosurgery, and at the age of 34 was one of the youngest directors of a surgical division in the United States. In 1987, a pair of German Siamese twins was born that were joined at the back of their heads. Dr. Carson designed the landmark operation, which involved 70 doctors and five months of planning and training. The operation lasted 22 hours, during which Dr. Carson and his team successfully separated the twins.

Ben Carson is very humble and gives God the glory. He's been quoted as saying, "God, I'm not going to be a neurosurgeon anymore. I'm going to be an assistant. You can be the neurosurgeon." Carson has written several books, including *Gifted Hands; Think Big;* and *The Big Picture: Getting Perspective on What's Really Important in Life.* He was inducted into the Academy of Surgeons in 1995.

Ben is married and they have three children.

Dr. Alexa Canady
(1950–)
NEUROSURGEON

Alexa Canady was born in Lansing, Michigan. She and her brother were the only African American students in the local elementary school. Her father was a highly respected dentist and her mother was a graduate of Fisk. Her high school academic accomplishment earned her the National Achievement Scholar in 1967.

Canady enrolled in the University of Michigan and earned a bachelor's degree in 1971. She was admitted to the College of Medicine and was elected into the Alpha Omega Alpha Honorary Medical Society. In 1975, she earned her M.D. degree and graduated cum laude. She interned at New Haven Hospital–Yale and in 1976, took a historic appointment as the first female and African American in neurosurgery at the University of Minnesota.

She remained there until 1981, and after successful completion, moved to Children's Hospital in Philadelphia. After two years, she moved back to Michigan. She became head of the pediatric neurosurgery department at Children's Hospital of Michigan. She is also a clinical associate professor at Wayne State University in Detroit.

Dr. Keith Black

(1957–)

NEUROSURGEON

Black was born in Tuskegee, Alabama, during the turbulent years of George Wallace's governorship. Though life was sometimes difficult for Blacks in Alabama, Black was provided with a solid foundation by his parents, particularly his father. Robert Black was an educator who would not allow limits to be placed on his students—especially his sons—due to their race or background. He was the principal of a local elementary school.

Black's family moved to Ohio when he was in junior high school. His favorite hangout spot became the research labs at Case Western Reserve University. By high school, the young student was getting a very early start for his surgical career by transplanting organs and replacing heart valves in dogs. Black's first love, however, was understanding the workings of the brain. He refers to this organ as "the most beautiful thing you'll ever see."

Black finished a six-year program at the University of Michigan in 1981 in biomedical science and medicine. He was an intern and resident at the University of Michigan Hospital from 1981–1987. Black became a professor of neurosurgery at UCLA in 1987. In the summer of 1997, Black accepted the position of Los Angeles's new neurosurgeon institute at Cedars-Sinai Medical Center. Part of Black's success as a surgeon lies in his great respect for the brain. While performing operations, Dr. Black takes great pains not to touch the brain itself—only the cancerous tumor he is trying to remove. Black's skills are also enhanced by the great technological advancements in medicine.

Dr. Black pioneered research on ways to open the blood-brain barrier, enabling chemotherapeutic drugs to be delivered directly into the tumor. He also is involved in developing a vaccine to enhance the body's immune response to brain tumors. He has published more than 100 scientific articles and presented research at more than 200 meetings worldwide.

Presently, there are only about fifty neurosurgeons in the United States, who specialize in the study and removal of brain tumors. Dr. Keith Black is among the very best in the world. Most of these fifty specialists average 100 surgeries per year. Because of his advanced skill and delicate technique, Dr. Black is among a very small minority who averages about 250 operations per year. Black has been called on to assist patients not only in America but as far away as Australia, the Middle East, Japan, Europe, and South America. Black has received numerous awards.

Despite his hectic schedule, Dr. Black finds time to cater to his love of adventure and travel. Referred to as "Indiana Black" by those who know him, Black has climbed mountains and rafted on rivers. Dr. Black lives with his wife, a urologist, and two children in Los Angeles.

COMMUNITY ACTIVISM, POLITICS, GOVERNMENT, AND LAW

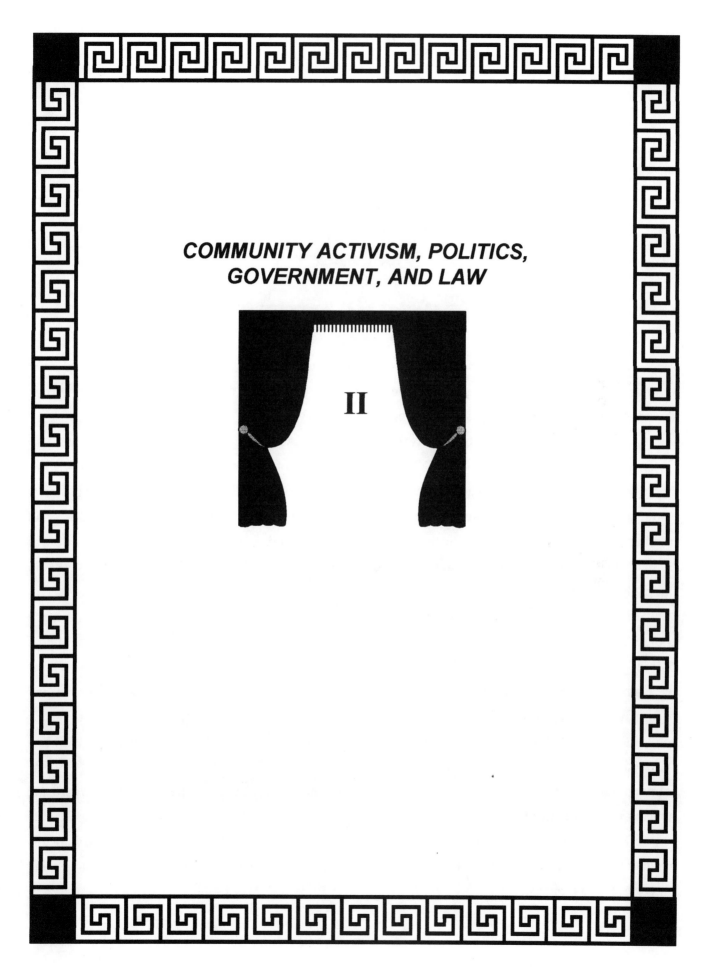

II

Fannie Lou Hamer

(1917–1977)

ACTIVIST

Fannie Lou Hamer was born in Montgomery County in Mississippi along with nineteen other siblings. When she was only six years old she was picking cotton with her sharecropping family. When she was thirteen, Hamer could pick 400 pounds of cotton per day.

Hamer's strong Christian beliefs drove her to fight injustice. In 1962, she joined SCLC (Southern Christian Leadership Council) and SNCC (Student NonViolent Coordinating Committee) and was inspired by Reverend James Bevel and James Foreman. Their first objective was securing the right to vote. She successfully registered to vote, passing the literacy test. Her sharecropping landowner was upset and told her to withdraw her voting application. Hamer told him, "I didn't register for you." Her house was riddled with bullets. Employment was difficult to find as a registered voter. She became a field-worker in the civil rights movement.

Her next challenge was dismantling Jim Crow laws. She and a group of workers sat at a lunch counter in the White section of a bus terminal in Winona, Mississippi. They were arrested, and the sheriff ordered two Black male prisoners to beat her with a black leather clutch loaded with metal. The incident left Hamer permanently injured, but they could not break her spirit. Her famous phrase was "I'm sick and tired of being sick and tired." Her next conquest was challenging the Mississippi Democratic Party's refusal to allow Black participation. She joined the Mississippi Freedom Democratic Party in 1964 and received national media attention. She was a delegate to the 1968 Democratic convention. In 1969, she founded the Freedom Farm, and fed 1,500 people with their crops. Homer helped provide day care and housing to many poor residents.

Hamer challenged sexism in SCLC, SNCC, and the Black church. She received honorary doctorate degrees from Shaw, Tougaloo, Howard, Morehouse, and Columbia in Chicago. She was married and they adopted two girls.

Stokely Carmichael–Kwame Ture
(1941–1998)
ACTIVIST

Kwame Ture was born in Trinidad, reared in Cuba and the United States, and died in Guinea. Ture could not be confined to a region, and his thoughts could not be controlled by oppressive forces. He was intelligent, articulate, energetic, and committed to the liberation of African people.

Ture was a student at Howard University in 1960, where he immersed himself in the liberation movement. The first organization he joined was SNCC (Student Nonviolent Coordinating Committee). This group of college students protested against racism and discrimination. They sat in at lunch counters and conducted freedom rides on interstate segregated buses. SNCC and SCLC (Southern Christian Leadership Council), led by Martin Luther King, collaborated on many of these efforts. Ture was jailed 39 times in his attempt to bring dignity to his people.

In 1966, Ture shared some of his ideological differences with Martin Luther King and his following. Ture wanted to change the slogan from "we shall overcome" to "Black Power." This debate reflects the historical conflicts between integrationists and nationalists. In 1966, Stokely Carmichael shouted in defiance of King on national television, "Black Power!" He went on to become a member of the Black Panther Party. He was constantly searching and growing.

Ture founded the AAPRP (All African People Revolutionary Party). He became a highly sought after speaker, not only in the United States, but in Central and South America and Africa. Ture understood the global oppression of African people and recognized that it would require global solutions.

In his fiery speeches, Ture would admonish his listeners to become a member of an organization. He felt African people were victims because they were not organized. He was so committed that he even answered the telephone by saying, "ready for the revolution."

On his death bed, Ture was still trying to empower his people by attempting to secure reconciliation between Minister Louis Farrakhan of the Nation of Islam and Julian Bond, chairman of the NAACP.

He is survived by two sons.

Angela Davis
(1944–)
ACTIVIST

Angela Davis was born in Birmingham, Alabama. She was negatively affected almost two decades later when four Black girls were bombed in a church. She and her three siblings were raised by parents who were schoolteachers. She observed her mother earning her master's degree during the summers.

There were so many homes bombed in her neighborhood of Birmingham that it was called "Dynamite Hill." In 1961, she earned a scholarship to Brandeis University to study French literature. She spent one year abroad, studying at the Sorbonne at the University of Paris. There she met students from Algeria and other African nations under colonial rule. She returned to Brandeis and learned Marxism from a professor of philosophy.

Davis graduated magna cum laude in 1965 and attended graduate school at the University of Frankfurt in Germany. She returned to the United States and completed her master's degree at the University of California at San Diego in 1968. While pursuing her doctoral studies, Angela Davis joined the Student Nonviolent Coordinating Committee (SNCC), the Black Panthers, and the Che-Lumumba Club, an all Black Communist collective in Los Angeles.

She was accused of providing guns in prison to the Soledad Brothers. A county judge was killed. Davis was placed on the FBI's Ten Most Wanted List. Angela was held in prison for a year. A national Free Angela movement took place. She was tried and found innocent by a jury in 1972.

The Communist Party nominated her as vice president in 1980 and 1984. She continues to be active in many organizations, including the National Alliance against Racist and Political Repression, which she founded, the National Political Congress of Black Women, and the National Black Women's Health Project. She continues to teach at one of many University of California Schools, including San Francisco State and Santa Cruz.

She is a highly sought after speaker and has written many books, including *Women, Race, and Class; Women, Culture, and Politics;* and *Blues Legacies and Black Feminism.*

Maulana Karenga
(1941–)
ACTIVIST, EDUCATOR, AND AUTHOR

Maulana Karenga was born in Parsonsburg, Maryland, to a Baptist minister. He pursued his education at Los Angeles City College and became the first African American to serve as president. He earned a master's degree and two doctorates at the University of California, one in social ethics and the other in political science.

He became immersed in the Black Power movement of the 1960s. He founded the US organization in 1965 and provided direction to the community after the riots in Watts, California. Karenga's influence was changed considerably after the killing of two Black Panther members by US gunmen in 1969. Karenga was arrested and convicted in 1971 for assaulting a female U.S. member.

Karenga felt the major problem facing Black people was cultural. He developed the theory Kawaida (tradition and reason), which encompassed the Nguzo Saba (seven principles of Blackness—unity, self-determination, collective work and responsibility, cooperative economics, purpose, creativity, and faith). The holiday Kwanzaa (first fruits) was created in 1966, and is celebrated from December 26 to January 1. It is the only non-hero African American holiday and is celebrated by millions of Africans worldwide. A Kwanzaa stamp was created in 1998.

Karenga won his freedom in 1974 with the support of community and political leaders. He returned to the Black Power movement and tried to learn from past mistakes. He founded Sankore Press, which is an Africentric publishing company. He has written numerous books, including *Kwanzaa: A Celebration of Family; Introduction to Black Studies; Kawaida Theory; Selections from the Husia; Reconstructing Kemetric Culture; The Book of Coming Faith by Day, Odu Ifa (The Ethical Teachings)* and many others.

He is actively involved in the Black United Front, Association for the Study of Classical African Civilization, the Million Man March Committee, Brotherhood Crusade, and many more. He is the chairman of the Black Studies Department at California State University at Long Beach. He is a highly sought after speaker.

He is married to Tiamoya, who has been involved with him in the struggle for liberation since 1967.

Marian Wright Edelman
(1939–)
ACTIVIST

Marian Wright Edelman was born in Bennettsville, South Carolina, the youngest of five children. She was named after Marian Anderson. Her father, who was a major influence on her life, was a minister. He exposed his children to positive role models when they came to town and stressed the need to work in the community.

Edelman attended Spelman College and studied in Russia. She was the valedictorian of her 1960 class. She wanted to become a civil rights lawyer and entered Yale University. She graduated in 1963 and became the first African American woman to pass the bar exam in Mississippi at the young age of twenty-six.

Edelman moved to Washington to study and make laws to empower poor people. This endeavor was called the Washington Research Project. This evolved into the Children's Defense Fund (CDF) in 1973. Under her leadership, CDF has become one of the nation's most effective organizations to rally people and shape public policy. She has become an effective lobbyist.

Edelman realized the tremendous impact that teenage pregnancy and out-of-wedlock births have had on the Black community. She is a strong proponent of Head Start, child care, and an adequate living wage to defeat poverty.

In 1996, CDF spearheaded a march called Stand for Children. More than 200,000 converged on Washington demanding more governmental support for children. She was very close to Alex Haley and CDF acquired his estate in Tennessee. The facility is designed to prepare young leaders and teach Black history and the quest for freedom.

Edelman has written several best-selling books, including *Measure for Success, Guide My Feet, Stand for Children*, and *Memoir of Mentors*. She was the first African American and second woman to chair the Board of Trustees of Spelman College. She has received hundreds of awards and more than forty honorary doctorates.

She is married and has three sons.

Dick Gregory
(1932–)
ACTIVIST

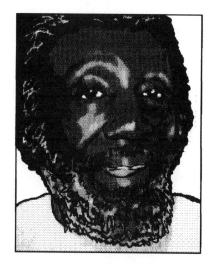

Dick Gregory has been running for something for his entire life. He was born in St. Louis and raised by his mother. They were so poor that Gregory joined the high school track team so that he could enjoy a hot shower. He excelled in track, became captain of the team, was the state champion in 1950, and won a scholarship to Southern Illinois University. Later in his life he would run marathons and march hundreds of miles for political reasons.

Gregory has always been articulate and entertaining. In 1959, he became the master of ceremonies at the famed Roberts Show Club in Chicago and learned from the likes of Nipsey Russell and Sammy Davis, Jr. In 1961, his agent booked him in the Playboy Club and his career skyrocketed. He was featured in *Time* and was a guest on the *Tonight Show* and *Jack Paar*. He became the first African American comedian to break the color barrier and perform for White audiences.

The key to his success was his satirical approach to race relations. This led Gregory into politics. He ran for the mayor of Chicago in 1966. Gregory received 200,000 votes in 1968 in his presidential candidacy.

Inspired by Martin Luther King, Jr., Gregory participated in many marches and protests. He would often fast to draw more attention to the issues of injustice. He has written several books, including *From the Back of the Bus, What's Happening? The Shadow That Scares Me, Write Me In! No More Lies, Dick Gregory's Political Primer, Dick Gregory's Natural Diet for Folks Who Eat, Dick Gregory's Bible Tales, Up From Nigger,* and *Code Name Zorro.*

Gregory left a very lucrative entertainment career for political and health reasons. He is a sought-after public speaker. He became a vegetarian and researched the relationship between diet and health. He created Dick Gregory Health Enterprises, which produced the successful Bahamian diet mixture.

Gregory resides in Plymouth, Massachusetts, with his wife. They have raised ten children.

Faye Wattleton
(1943–)
ACTIVIST

Faye Wattleton was born an only child in St. Louis, Missouri. Her family was poor, but the value of education was stressed. At the age of sixteen, she enrolled in Ohio State School of Nursing. She graduated in 1964. Her first professional job was as a maternity nursing instructor. In 1966, she moved to New York to attend Columbia University. There she earned her master's degree in maternal and infant health care in 1967.

Wattleton has strong beliefs about pro-choice. Once when interning in Harlem, she learned that a mother had decided to give her daughter an abortion by inserting a Lysol douche into her uterus. The young woman was killed. Faye Wattleton joined Planned Parenthood in Dayton, Ohio, in 1967. The organization appreciated her zeal and compassion. Wattleton was rewarded with the Dayton Executive Director position. Under her leadership the number of clients tripled and budgets increased from $400,000 to $1 million. In 1973, she became the National Director. She was the first Black and female to hold this position. At thirty years old she was also one of the youngest.

Wattleton was a tireless worker. She organized, met, and spoke with anyone concerned about sex education and pro-choice. Her major obstacles were the Hyde Amendment, which blocked Medicaid as a source for funding abortions. The Supreme Court's ruling in Webster vs. Reproduction Health Services gave states the right to limit access to abortion.

Wattleton has written two books, *How to Talk to Your Child about Sex* and *Life on the Line*. In 1993 she was inducted into the Women's Hall of Fame. She has received more than fifteen honorary doctorate degrees. Although she is no longer the president of Planned Parenthood, she remains active, visible, and vocal. She is the founder and directs the Center for Gender Equality. She has one daughter.

Medgar Evers

(1925–1963)

ACTIVIST

Medgar Evers was born July 2, 1925, in Decatur, Mississippi, to strongly religious parents. Evers' father was a farmer and sawmill operator, and his mother was a domestic worker who took in ironing. Evers attended a one-room elementary school in Decatur, and then later, walked twelve miles to high school in nearby Newton.

In 1946, after serving in Normandy during World War II, he returned home and enrolled in Alcorn A & M College, where he majored in business administration and got a job as the school newspaper editor. While there, he met and married his wife Myrlie.

Following college, in 1952, he got a job selling life insurance, but quit soon after to join the NAACP and the growing civil rights movement. In 1954, he became the NAACP's Mississippi field secretary. After the *Brown vs. The Board of Education* Supreme Court ruling outlawing public school segregation that year, Evers actively sought enforcement of that ruling in his state, which had one of the most rigid systems of segregation in the country.

In 1962, Evers played a key role in enrolling James Meredith as the first Black student at the University of Mississippi, a major victory in the early stages of the civil rights movement. Evers went on to spearhead a number of economic boycotts of businesses that practiced segregation in downtown Jackson. He also helped form the Jackson Movement, an umbrella of Black organizations that sponsored mass demonstrations throughout the state. The group demanded integration of all public facilities and institutions, and increased job opportunities for Blacks on city payrolls. However, at the time, opposition to the civil rights movements was perhaps at its most entrenched and violent, especially in Mississippi.

As Evers returned home the evening of June 12, 1963, he was shot in the back by Byron De La Beckwith, a fertilizer salesman and member of an old Mississippi family. It took three trials and thirty years before Beckwith was finally found guilty and convicted of Evers' murder. The 1996 film *Ghosts of Mississippi*, starring Whoopi Goldberg and James Woods, portrays the tears that were shed and the turmoil that was faced during the trial.

Evers' death was the first murder of a nationally known civil rights leader, which showed the world the degree to which racial violence was practiced in the South. It sparked more participation in the movement by outraged Americans, which led to even more demonstrations and violence. His death was a motivating factor in President John F. Kennedy's decision, one week later, to ask Congress to enact comprehensive civil rights legislation.

Medgar Evers was one of the civil rights movement's most important martyrs. He was murdered at the age of 38 and was buried in Arlington National Cemetery with full military honors. He is survived by a wife and four children.

Myrlie Evers-Williams
(1933–)
ACTIVIST

Myrlie Beasley was born in Vicksburg, Mississippi. The child of a teenaged, unwed mother, Myrlie was raised by her grandmother and her aunt. Both women were educators and therefore highly respected within the community. Despite her precarious life, Myrlie was given high expectations. Myrlie was an honor student who learned to sing, play the piano, and recite poetry. After high school, Myrlie enrolled in Alcorn A&M College in Lorman, Mississippi. On her first day at Alcorn, the wide-eyed, nervous freshman met a handsome, athletic upperclassman who she thought was named Edgar. The rest was history. Myrlie Louise Beasley married Medgar Evers on Christmas Eve, 1951.

The young couple moved to Mound Bayou, Mississippi. Medgar's work on behalf of Black people in Mississippi kept the family in constant danger. On June 12, 1963, their worst nightmare came true, when Medgar Evers was gunned down on the family's front porch.

Myrlie Evers was now a widow and single mother with very young children. She was pregnant with a fifth child when Medgar Evers was killed, but she later miscarried. She did not want her children to grow up amid the hatred of Mississippi and the traumatic setting of their father's death, so she moved to California, where she completed her bachelor's degree. She also traveled around the country speaking to NAACP audiences about her late husband's work in Mississippi.

In the 1970s, Evers entered corporate America. She worked as vice president at an advertising agency. In 1975, she became the national director for ARCO, one of Fortune 500's top fifteen companies. Her performance earned her a promotion to director of Consumer Affairs.

Evers remarried in 1976. Despite her busy schedule, she still found time to try her hand at politics. She ran for Congress in the 70s and for the Los Angeles City Council in 1987. That same year, Mayor Tom Bradley appointed her to the Los Angeles Board of Public Works. Evers was a full-time commissioner until 1995. That same year, Evers was elected chairperson of the NAACP, a position she held until 1998.

In addition to all of her professional accomplishments, Evers-Williams celebrated an enormous personal victory when Byron De La Beckwith was found guilty in 1994 of Medgar Evers' murder thirty years earlier. The movie *Ghosts of Mississippi* describes her ordeal. Evers-Williams 1999 biography *Watch Me Fly: What I Learned On Becoming the Woman I Was Meant To Be* details her struggle and eventual triumph.

Jesse Jackson, Sr.
(1941–)
ACTIVIST

Jesse Jackson was born in Greenville, South Carolina, the offspring of an unwed high school mother. The family was so poor, they didn't even have indoor plumbing until Jackson was in sixth grade. Poverty, however, was not an obstacle to success. Jackson was president of his high school class, and earned academic and athletic scholarships to the University of Illinois. He left due to racism and enrolled at North Carolina A&T. He again became president of the class and enjoyed being mentored by President Samuel Proctor.

Jackson graduated in 1964 and joined Dr. King in 1965. He was involved in many marches, including the one at Selma. Dr. King saw much potential in Jackson, and he became a trusted aide. King appointed Jackson to head Operation Breadbasket in 1966. Operation Breadbasket was the economic arm of the Southern Christian Leadership Council (SCLC). One objective of Operation Breadbasket was to induce White businesses to carry Black-owned products. He attended Chicago Theological Seminary and was ordained by the Reverend Clay Evans in 1968.

In 1971, Jackson resigned from SCLC. Jackson founded PUSH (People United to Save Humanity). PUSH Excel was created to help improve academic excellence by encouraging greater parental involvement and more study time.

Jackson became a national leader. While criticized for his lack of follow-up, no one brought more attention to an issue than Jackson. He could not be confined to Chicago or the country. In 1979 he negotiated the release of Lieutenant Robert Goodman in the Middle East. He was active in the politics of South Africa and Cuba. He campaigned for the presidency in 1984 and 1988. He won 3.5 million votes in 1984 and doubled the figure in 1988. He won South Carolina and four other southern states and stunned the nation when he won Michigan. No politician has registered more voters or inspired so many to extend their dreams to the White House.

Jackson moved to Washington and was sworn in as the Shadow Senator in 1991. He founded the National Rainbow Coalition in 1984 to continue his quest to organize African Americans, women, Asians, Latinos, Native Americans, and poor Whites. In 1995 he returned to Chicago to strengthen Operation PUSH. His son and namesake, Jesse Jackson, Jr., has become a Congressman. The remaining two sons have become astute businessmen and work with their father on the Wall Street Project, Jackson's response to Texaco and boardroom racism. President Clinton appointed Jackson special envoy to Africa. Clinton was the first president to visit Africa. Jackson has provided spiritual consultation to the First Family.

Jackson hosts a weekly television talk show on CNN. He is a much sought after speaker. Jackson has received thousands of awards. He is married with five children.

Dorothy Irene Height
(1912–)
ACTIVIST

Dorothy Irene Height was born in Richmond, Virginia. Her family moved to the small mining town of Rankin, Pennsylvania, where, as a tall, straight-A student, Height excelled in athletics. Active even as a teenager at the YWCA, she continues to contribute to them. She attended New York University, earning both her bachelor's and her master's degrees in four years. She also studied at Columbia University and the New York School of Social Work.

She helped Eleanor Roosevelt plan a 1938 World Youth Congress in New York. At the same time, she worked for New York's Welfare Department, examining the unrest following the 1935 riots in Harlem. During that period, she met with the founder of the National Council of Negro Women (NCNW) and civil rights activist Mary McLeod Bethune, and began volunteering in the group's quest for women's rights.

Height began her long career with the Young Women's Christian Association in 1938, running a lodging home for African American women in Harlem and later in Washington, D.C. She also ran training programs for YWCA volunteers and developed programs for interracial education. Height eventually helped desegregate the YWCA membership. She later directed its Center for Racial Justice.

In 1939, Height began her tenure with Delta Sigma Theta Sorority, guiding the national African American sorority toward a greater commitment to activism. She was national president from 1947 and served until 1956, during which time she established the sorority's first international chapter in Haiti. During her term in office she organized bookmobiles for African American communities in the South.

Shortly afterward, Height took on the position of president of National Council of Negro Women (NCNW), an umbrella group for women's rights organizations. The council's goals include uniting African American women of all classes and stressing interracial cooperation. During her tenure, the council has helped women open businesses, sponsored job training, and run voter registration programs. Height continues to guide the fight for equal rights for women of color worldwide. In 1986, the council began sponsoring annual celebrations nationwide known as Black Family Reunions, which is an attempt to renew the concept of the extended Black family and to improve social conditions.

Dorothy Irene Height is the recipient of numerous awards and honorary degrees and continues to be a firebrand in the struggle to improve the lives of Blacks and women.

Queen Mother Audley Moore
(1898–1997)
ACTIVIST

Queen Mother Audley Moore was born in New Iberia, Louisiana. The family moved to New Orleans, where she heard and met Marcus Garvey. She was greatly influenced by his views on Pan Africanism and economic empowerment. She became a life member of Garvey's Universal Negro Improvement Association (UNIA).

Queen Mother moved to Harlem and noticed that oppression in the North was the same as in the South. She became active in the Communist party and spearheaded rent strikes against racist absentee landlords. She also worked with Mary McLeod Bethune and the National Council of Negro Women (NCNW). She was critical of W. E. B. DuBois and the Pan African Congress because they excluded women in their first two conferences in 1919 and 1921. She was just as critical of Elijah Muhammad, who was unreceptive to female leadership and was reluctant to establish ties with Africa. She resigned from the Communist party in 1950 and accused them of being racist to the core.

In the 1950s she became a major spokesperson for reparations. She organized and directed the Reparations Committee of the Descendants of United States Slaves. She met with John F. Kennedy about the matter. Queen Mother Moore founded the African American Cultural Foundation and promoted the term African American over Black and Negro. She also founded the Ethiopian Orthodox Church of North and South America and the Republic of New Africa. She encouraged African Americans to visit Africa. In honor of her sister, she founded the Elouise Moore College of African Studies on a 200-acre plot of land in Mount Addis Ababa, New York. Her advice was sought by Malcolm X.

In 1972, the country of Ghana gave Moore the honorary title Queen Mother because of her work and commitment to the liberation of African people. At age 98, she attended the historic Million Man March in 1995. Her speech was read by her assistant.

Clara Hale
(1905–1992)
ACTIVIST

Clara Hale, the youngest of four children, was born in Philadelphia, Pennsylvania. Her father died when she was an infant, and her mother reared the children by providing rooms and meals to lodgers. Clara Hale moved to New York as an adult, married, and had three children. Her husband died at twenty-seven.

Influenced by her mother, who had also been a single parent, Mother Hale reared forty foster children before she retired in 1968. Her daughter Lorraine, who became a doctor, encountered a young female heroin addict with a two-month-old baby. She encouraged the addict to visit her mother. News spread that Mother Hale would take care of addicted babies.

Mother Hale had accepted more than 1,000 addicted babies and their mothers. Initially, the financial support came from her three children, but as word spread about this dynamic woman who had a heart like God's, the numbers increased. Percy Sutton, lawyer and entrepreneur, and others began to fund the project. The main objective of Hale House is to take drug-dependent children at birth, rear them until their mothers complete a drug treatment program, and reunite the mother and the child when the treatment ends. President Ronald Reagan acknowledged Mother Hale in his State of the Union address in 1985. John Jay College of Criminal Justice awarded her an honorary doctorate.

Betty Shabazz
(1936–1997)
ACTIVIST

Betty Shabazz grew up in Detroit and was adopted by a middle-class family. She was an only child. She attended the Brooklyn School of Nursing and met Malcolm X in New York in 1957. They "group" dated for several months, and Malcolm X proposed by telephone. They eloped because her family had concerns about the age and religious differences. She was 23 while Malcolm X was 32. He was a Muslim while she was a Christian.

They were married for only seven years when Malcolm X was assassinated in 1965 before her very eyes. They had four children at the time, and Betty was pregnant with twins. He died with less than $600 and no house. Attorney Percy Sutton and friends raised the money for the funeral, a house, and living expenses.

Betty Shabazz was committed to raising her children without going on welfare. She worked as a nurse and earned a bachelor's degree in public health from Jersey City State College and a Ph.D. from the University of Massachusetts in administration in 1975. She became a professor of health administration at Medgar Evers College in Brooklyn. She was a sought-after speaker and active in community affairs.

Her primary objective was the proper raising of her six daughters. They attended excellent schools, and she exposed them to international travel, foreign languages, ballet, and Black history. She provided nurturing and discipline.

In 1995, 30 years after Malcolm X was killed, Shabazz and Farrakhan spoke for the first time publicly and they shook hands in front of 1,400 people at the Apollo Theatre in Harlem, New York.

Shabazz's grandson Malcolm set her apartment on fire. She died of severe burns to her body on June 23, 1997.

Aileen Hernandez
(1926–)
ACTIVIST

Aileen Hernandez was born in Brooklyn, New York, the only daughter of Jamaican parents. She and her two brothers were taught that when it came to doing housework or school work, gender was irrelevant. This left an indelible impression on Aileen. She graduated from her high school as salutatorian and won a scholarship to Howard University, where she majored in political science.

She graduated in 1947 and pursued graduate studies at the University of Oslo, where she studied comparative government. She completed her master's degree at Los Angeles State College in 1959.

Hernandez was attracted to the labor movement. She became active in the International Ladies Garment Workers Union (ILGWU). During the 1960s she represented the State Department as a labor specialist and toured many South American countries. She was appointed assistant chief of the California Fair Employment Practice Commission. She supervised a staff of fifty. Lyndon Johnson appointed her as a commissioner to the Equal Employment Opportunity Commission (EEOC). Hernandez has said, "When they appoint me they get someone Black, who is a woman, with a Mexican-American last name, who comes from California, and has been involved in the labor movement."

In 1967, Hernandez became the first African American to become president of the National Organization of Women (NOW). The appointment came at a time when the Black Women's Movement did not trust NOW.

Hernandez also started her own public relations and management firm. She was able to leverage her contacts into a lucrative consulting company. She continues to lecture on civil rights and equal employment opportunities.

Ron Brown
(1941–1996)
SECRETARY OF COMMERCE

Ronald Harmon Brown was born on August 1, 1941, in Washington, D.C., to Bill and Gloria Brown. In the mid-1940s, Bill Brown moved his young family to Boston, where he was transferred by his employer. The family moved again in 1948, when Bill Brown became the manager of the renowned Theresa Hotel in Harlem. The hotel was frequented by positive African American role models. Although seven-year-old Ron was in awe of the people who passed through the hotel, this early exposure taught him to be comfortable in the presence of great leaders.

Brown's uncommon intelligence led to his enrollment in a predominantly White school for gifted children. This experience helped Ron learn to function effectively in different racial settings. After high school and his graduation from Middlebury College in 1962, Ron served in the Army in Germany and Korea until 1967.

In 1967, Brown was hired by the National Urban League, where he worked until 1979. He earned his law degree from St. John University in 1970. During this period, Brown worked closely with valuable mentors like Whitney Young and Vernon Jordan. Brown ventured deeper into the political arena when he served as deputy campaign manager for Ted Kennedy's presidential campaign. In 1988, Brown was asked to work as convention campaign manager for Jesse Jackson's historic presidential campaign. The following year marked a major milestone, when Brown was elected the first African American chairman of the Democratic National Committee (DNC).

Brown headed trade missions with American executives to five continents. These missions resulted in more than $80 million worth of foreign business for U.S. companies. On his last mission to Croatia in April 1996, Brown died in a plane crash. Ron Brown University in Dubrovnik, Croatia, stands as a testament to Brown's legacy. He is survived by a wife and two children. His daughter, Tracey wrote a book about him entitled—*The Life and Times of Ron Brown.*

31

Shirley Chisholm
(1924–)
CONGRESSWOMAN

Shirley Anita St. Hill Chisholm, born to Barbados immigrants in Brooklyn, New York, on November 30, 1924, became the first Black woman to serve in the United States Congress. Although Chisholm received scholarships from Vassar and Oberlin Colleges, she remained in Brooklyn, where she graduated with a degree in education from Brooklyn College in 1946. She later received her master's degree in early childhood development from Columbia University in 1952.

In 1953, Chisholm worked as a teacher and director of nursery schools and child care centers for working mothers, but left in 1959 to work as a consultant for the Bureau of Child Welfare. In 1964, she entered politics after being chosen to represent the Brooklyn residents in the New York state legislature. She joined the State Assembly and worked there until 1968. That same year, she was elected to the United States Congress and served in the House of Representatives for seven terms (from 1969 to 1983), being the first Black woman to do so. She campaigned for but did not win the 1972 Democratic presidential nomination, although she did win 10 percent of the Democratic Convention votes.

During her seven terms, she has advocated for women's rights, abortion reform, day care, environment protection, job training, and an end to the Vietnam War (1959 to 1975). She also spoke out against the seniority system in Congress and protested her 1969 assignment. She later won reassignment to a committee which she felt was of better service to the people of Brooklyn.

After declining to run for an eighth term in the House of Representatives in 1982, Chisholm became a professor at Mount Holyoke College in Massachusetts. Chisholm wrote two autobiographies: *Unbought and Unbossed* in 1970 and *The Good Fight* in 1973. Shirley Chisholm is married.

President Nelson Mandela
(1918–)
ACTIVIST

Nelson Mandela was born in the rural town of Umtata in South Africa. He was the son of a highly placed tribal advisor. After the death of his father in 1930, the 12-year-old impressed his elders, and many thought he would someday become chief. Mandela renounced his hereditary right to the tribal chieftain and entered college to pursue a law degree. He was expelled from the college at Fort Hare because he led a student strike. He did earn his law degree from the University of South Africa in 1942. He contemplated a boxing career.

Nelson joined the African National Congress (ANC) in 1944 and formed a sub-group—The Congress Youth League. Mandela led many labor strikes and other acts of protest against apartheid. Many were killed, and others were placed in jail. He went underground and the struggle continued. He formed a guerilla organization (Umkonto we Sizwe—Spear of the Nation) that engaged in sabotage against the government. He told his wife (Winnie Mandela), who was also very committed to the struggle, "Anticipate a life physically without me. There will never be a normal situation where I will be head of the family."

Every time he was indicted for a crime, he used his legal background to defend himself and illustrate the unfairness of apartheid. The government realized the unifying effect he had on his people and sentenced him to life imprisonment in June 1964. He was placed in Robben Island, where he spent eighteen years. Another nine years were spent at Pollsmoor. Although he utilized a large amount of time meeting with other political prisoners, most of his jail term was spent in solitary confinement. As a former athlete, he tried staying in shape and never lost faith. He was allowed to see his wife twice a year. Her letters were always opened prior to his receiving them.

In 1984, Mandela was offered a release if he would stay away from ANC activities and live in Transkei, a Black homeland. Mandela refused. On February 11, 1990, the world watched Mandela move from prisoner to president. He left under his own terms.

Unfortunately, he and Winnie divorced. The separation was too much for them to bear. President Mandela resigned from office in 1999. He has written several books, including *No Easy Walk to Freedom, Autobiography of Nelson Mandela*, and *The Struggle is My Life*. He was awarded the Noble Peace Prize in 1993. He married Graca Machel, the former wife of the Mozambique president, in 1998. Nelson Mandela has five children.

Barbara Jordan
(1936–1996)
POLITICIAN

Barbara Jordan was born and raised in segregated Houston, Texas. She was the youngest of three girls born to working class parents. She was a very good high school student, and in 1952, placed first in the state Oratorical Contest, won a trip to Chicago, and won the national contest.

Jordan attended Texas Southern University, where she joined the debate team. Harvard was unable to beat Jordan's debate team. She graduated and decided to forego law school to pursue a career in politics.

She campaigned for Kennedy and Johnson in 1960, organized Harris County in Texas, and produced an 80 percent voter turnout. This was the highest percentage ever produced. Jordan became a speaker for the Harris County Democratic Party. In 1962 and 1964, she lost in her bid for a House seat in the Texas Legislature. In 1965, after the district was reapportioned, she won a state senatorial seat. Jordan was the first African American elected since 1883 and the first woman ever. She decided to forego marriage because she felt politics and marriage was incompatible. She was well respected in the Texas Legislature.

In 1972, she became the first African American and the first woman to represent the state of state of Texas in the United States Congress. She received national attention as a member of the House Judiciary Committee which considered the impeachment of Richard Nixon. Her peers loved or hated her, but everyone respected her.

Jordan left Congress in 1978 to teach at the Lyndon B. Johnson School of Public Affairs, University of Texas at Austin. Jordan received numerous awards and more than twenty honorary doctorates. She was given the honor of being a major speaker at the Democratic National Conventions in 1976 and 1992. This was a first for an African American.

Jordan died of pneumonia in 1996 and was eulogized by President Bill Clinton and Texas governor Anne Richards.

Harold Washington
(1922–1987)
POLITICIAN

Harold Washington was born in Chicago, Illinois. His father was a lawyer and a Democratic precinct captain. Harold Washington would work with his father after school and on weekends. Ironically, the brilliant student dropped out of his school in his junior year due to boredom, but not before he won the city championship in the 110-yard high hurdles. Later this brilliant athlete would die because he was 100 pounds overweight.

Washington joined the Air Force during World War II and completed his GED. During the war, he became a serious student and after World War II, he enrolled at Roosevelt University. The 95 percent White student body elected him class president. He earned a bachelor's degree in 1949. Washington graduated from Northwestern Law School in 1952. He worked with his father in his law practice and Democratic politics. He fell in love with the political process.

He took issue with mayor Richard J. Daley's political machine, as it was called. For more than 21 years, the city was run on a patronage system that often excluded African Americans. Washington vowed to take on the machine. He was elected to the Illinois House of Representatives in 1965. He held that seat for six terms. When Daley died, Washington ran for mayor in 1977 and received only 11 percent of the vote. Washington was not dismayed. He won a state Senate seat in 1976 and later defeated the machine candidate for a U.S. Congressional seat in 1980. He was happy to be away from city politics and thought he would be a U.S. congressman forever.

The Black community had other plans. Black leaders promised Washington an increase in voter registration, voter turnout, and financial support. In 1983, Washington won with a record-setting Black turnout. The machine had been defeated. The White power structure maintained control of the city council and made passing legislation a nightmare. Washington endured for six years, but the stress, his weight, and overall declining health initiated a fatal heart attack. The Chicago Black community has yet to recover.

Maxine Waters
(1939–)
POLITICIAN

Maxine Waters was born the fifth of thirteen children in St. Louis, Missouri. She relocated to Los Angeles after high school and raised two children as a single parent. She became a community organizer for Head Start and rose to assistant teacher and director. She earned her bachelor's degree from UCLA in 1972.

Her love of politics began with Tom Bradley's run for mayor. In 1976, she ran for the California legislature and won. She initiated a ban on the state investing its pension funds in businesses operating in South Africa. Her mentor was Willie Brown, and she learned much from this dynamic politician. In 1990 she won a Congressional seat by winning 80 percent of the vote.

Waters is loved by her constituents. Gang members respect her. She created Project Build to provide career development for inner-city youth. She refused to call her constituents rioters in 1992, after the Rodney King beating and the acquittal of the involved police officers. She demanded resources from Washington to restore the community. She is very vocal about the onslaught of guns and drugs in her neighborhood. She believes it is part of a conspiracy to infiltrate the Black community. She is quick to bring media attention to injustices.

Her peers rewarded her by voting her chair of the Congressional Black Caucus in 1996. Waters wanted to use this platform to bring attention to urban problems. She is not afraid to debate decay any congressperson on any issue.

Waters serves in many organizations, including TransAfrica, which is led by her friend Randall Robinson. She is equally concerned about the empowerment of Cuba and the ban against the country being lifted.

Waters has received numerous awards and remains a tireless worker who is willing to fly coast to coast to empower her people. Waters is married with two children.

Alexis Herman
(1947–)
SECRETARY OF LABOR

Alexis Herman was born and raised in Mobile, Alabama, and graduated from Xavier University in New Orleans in 1969. She began her professional career in 1969 when she became the director of the Minority Women's Employment Program. At the age of 29, she became the youngest director of the Women's Bureau of the Department of Labor.

Herman served as the chief of staff for the Democratic National Committee in 1989 and as deputy chair in 1991. She has served on numerous boards and received hundreds of awards.

Her shining moment was being approved by the Congress to serve as Secretary of Labor in 1997. President Clinton had nominated her months prior but racism, sexism, and a Republican controlled congress showed their ugly heads.

The first African American woman to serve as Secretary of Labor said in Essence magazine, "It's important that we set high goals for ourselves. It never occurred to me that I couldn't be anything I wanted to be."

Herman knew she had two decades of labor experience. She also knew she had the concern of working people in labor negotiations. Since approved, Herman has received nothing but praise from both colleagues and adversaries. She was magnificent in helping resolve the labor dispute between truck drivers and UPS. Her nickname, "Queen of Smooth," reflects her ability to get both sides to talk to each other.

Admiral J. Paul Reason
(1941–)
ADMIRAL

J. Paul Reason is the son of a mother who was a biology teacher and a father who was library director at Howard University. Reason had the second-highest score on a high school ROTC exam. But due to racism, he was denied entrance into the Naval Academy. However, Reason was not deterred. He pursued his education at Howard and earned his bachelor's degree. He finally was admitted to the Naval Academy and earned a master's degree in Computer Systems Management. He continued his education in nuclear engineering. He studied defense policy at the Kennedy School of Government at Harvard University.

Reason's hard work, perseverance, and stellar educational background earned him the honor in 1996, of being the first African American four-star admiral. His responsibilities on the U.S. Atlantic govern the North Pole to the South Pole, the Caribbean Sea and waters around Central and South America, Norway, Greenland, and the waters around Africa down to the Cape of Good Hope. In addition, he is responsible for 125,000 active sailers, 191 ships, 1,300 aircrafts, and a $5 billion budget.

Admiral Reason wants to upgrade the Navy to twenty-first century standards. He feels the Navy is using World War II operations. He believes a greater infusion of technology could reduce the number of military personnel.

The 6-foot-5 210 pounder is known as the "gentle giant" by his Navy colleagues. He is married and has two children. His son is a lieutenant in the Navy.

Carol Mosely Braun

(1947–)

POLITICIAN

Carol Mosely Braun was born in Chicago, the eldest of four children. She graduated in 1967 from the University of Illinois at Chicago with a bachelor's degree and earned a law degree from the University of Chicago Law School in 1972.

Her public career began in 1974 as an assistant U.S. Attorney. In 1977, she won a seat in the Illinois House of Representatives as a Democrat. Braun championed educational reform, a ban against investing in South Africa and sued her own party over redistricting for fairer representation. She received the Best Legislator Award in 1980 and 1982 from the Independent Voters of Illinois. She was appointed floor leader by Mayor Harold Washington in 1983, over senior legislators. In 1988 she became the first African American elected to an executive office in the history of Cook County government. The coveted position was Recorder of Deeds, which had a budget of $8 million and a staff of 300 people.

Braun was inspired to run for the U.S. Senate when Senator Alan Dixon voted to confirm Clarence Thomas as a Supreme Court Justice in 1991. An African American woman had never won a Senate seat. The incumbent, Alan Dixon, had not lost a race in forty-three years. The stage was set. Her other Democratic opponent, Alfred Hofeld, spent $5 million, Dixon spent $2 million, and Carol only $350,000. While Dixon and Hofeld fought, Braun breezed past them with her charisma, intelligence, and an appealing platform. Women, who were tired of having no representation in the male-dominated Congress, came out in droves, and Braun won decisively.

Senator Braun's excellent performance in her first two years earned her an appointment in January 1995 to the powerful Finance Committee. She was the first woman ever appointed. She fought for and won for the removal of a symbol on the confederate flag. She became the education Senator, advocating for equal funding and new construction for all districts.

Unfortunately, Senator Braun lost in her bid for a second term. The combination of personal and fiscal issues and again being outspent by $10 million by her opponent produced defeat. Braun remains resilient and has options of a position in the Department of Education, becoming an Ambassador, the lecture circuit, and becoming a professor. She has one son.

Colin Powell
(1937–)
GENERAL

Colin Luther Powell was born at the end of the Great Depression. The son of Jamaican immigrants, Powell grew up in Harlem and South Bronx sections of New York City. When Powell was growing up, his father worked as a foreman in the shipping department for a garment district firm, and his mother worked as a seamstress. Powell attended P.S. 39 elementary school and Morris High School in the Bronx. He graduated from the City College of New York in 1958.

When in school, Powell grew to like the discipline of the Reserve Officers Training Corps (ROTC). Upon graduation, in 1958, he had already been commissioned second lieutenant. He went on to continue his training in the South, where in Birmingham, AL, he met and married Alma Johnson. Shortly thereafter, he left the country and served twice in Vietnam during the Vietnam War as head advisor in 1962-63 and in the army's 23rd division in 1968-69.

During the war, while Powell was leading a combat unit near the North Vietnamese border, his son was born. A week later, while patrolling near the Laotian border, he came across a booby-trap and was severely wounded after stepping on a punji stick that drove all the way through his left foot. Powell received a Purple Heart upon his discharge.

He received an MBA degree from George Washington University in Washington D.C. in 1971. He enrolled in the prestigious U.S. Army's Command and General Staff College. In 1972, he took his first political position as a White House fellow, and soon became an assistant in the Defense department.

Over the years, he held various positions in the Pentagon and elsewhere, starting in 1983, when he became Secretary of Defense Casper Weinberger's Senior Military Assistant. In 1986, he was promoted to Commanding General of the Fifth corps in Frankfurt, Germany. In 1987, he joined the staff of the National Security Council as the first African-American Deputy Council Chief. That same year, President Ronald Reagan named him Assistant to the President for National Security Affairs. Later, Reagan appointed him President. In 1989, Powell took over the Armed Forces Command, and became a four star general. In August of that year, President George Bush nominated him Chairman of the Joint Chiefs of Staff. This is the highest military advisory group and the chairman is the principal military advisor to the president. Powell became the first African American to hold that position. As chairman, he played a leading role in planning the invasion in Panama in 1989, and emerged from Operation Desert Storm an American hero. In 1991, he won the Springarn Medal from the NAACP, and retired from the military in September of 1993.

After the release of his best-selling autobiography, *My American Journey* in 1995, Powell flirted with the idea of campaigning for the presidency. He ultimately changed his mind deciding the time just wasn't right. In 1997, he coordinated the largest contingent of volunteers for the project—Volunteer America. He has solicited corporate support and plans to continue this massive effort.

He is married and they have three children.

Johnnie Cochran
(1938–)
LAWYER

Johnnie Cochran was born in Shreveport, Louisiana, and his family moved to Los Angeles when he was six years old. He attended college prep schools and graduated from UCLA in 1959 and Loyola Law School in 1962. He was appointed to the American College of Trial Lawyers, an honor reserved for the top 1 percent of attorneys in the country.

Cochran's list of clients reads like a list of the rich and famous. It includes Michael Jackson, Todd Bridges, Jim Brown, Latrelle Sprewell, and O.J. Simpson. Cochran's last client catapulted his fame as the country observed this brilliant legal mind. The country was obsessed with the O.J. Simpson case. In years past, if a Black man had harmed a White woman, there would have been a lynching. The White citizenry wanted to legally lynch Simpson, but Johnnie Cochran and the Dream Team successfully proved reasonable doubt.

Cochran had years of preparation before the O.J. Simpson case. His career began as a L. A. Public Defender. He understood the harassment of Los Angeles Police Department. Over the years, Cochran has won more than $45 million in claims against the department and had the infamous chokehold outlawed in the city.

Cochran founded his own law firm to represent not only the rich and famous but also the least of these, including political prisoner, Geronimo Pratt and police brutality victim, Abner Louima. The late U.S. Supreme Court Justice Thurgood Marshall is his role model. He has also become a sports agent and talk show host. His best-selling book is *Journey to Justice*. He is married with three children.

Willie Gary
(1947–)
LAWYER

Willie Gary was born the sixth of eleven children to farming parents in Eastman, Georgia. He was raised in Indiantown, Florida, and worked in the cane fields. He earned a bachelor's degree from Shaw University in 1971 and a Juris Doctor from the North Carolina Central University law school in 1974.

Gary relocated to Florida in 1975 and opened his own law firm. He is considered one of the best lawyers in the country. Over the past two decades, he has lost only three cases. His law firm averages 7,000 cases annually, with a staff of thirty attorneys and 100 other employees.

The media discovered Gary in 1995, when he won a $500 million judgment on behalf of a Mississippi funeral home against the unscrupulous business tactics of the Loewen Group in Canada. This was the third-largest jury verdict in United States history. The case was settled for $175 million. Gary went on to successfully sue tobacco companies in Mississippi.

Gary, a staunch Christian who pumps gospel music throughout his house and office, is launching a gospel music cable television network. He is driven by the scripture, "To whom much is given, much is required." Gary has contributed $10 million to his alma mater, Shaw University, and hundreds of thousands of dollars to many other colleges and foundations. He serves as a board member and trustee to many universities. He has received more than ten honorary doctor of law degrees. He has won hundreds of awards and is Jesse Jackson, Sr.'s personal attorney. He has also invested in many business ventures.

Gary flies from coast to coast in his private Gulfstream eighteen-passenger jet named "Wings of Justice." The plane is also used to transport cancer patients to treatment centers. He now lives in a $10 million, three-level, 25,000 square foot mansion in Florida just thirty minutes from the three-room cabin that he shared with his ten siblings.

Gary is married and has four sons, two of whom are completing law school.

EDUCATION

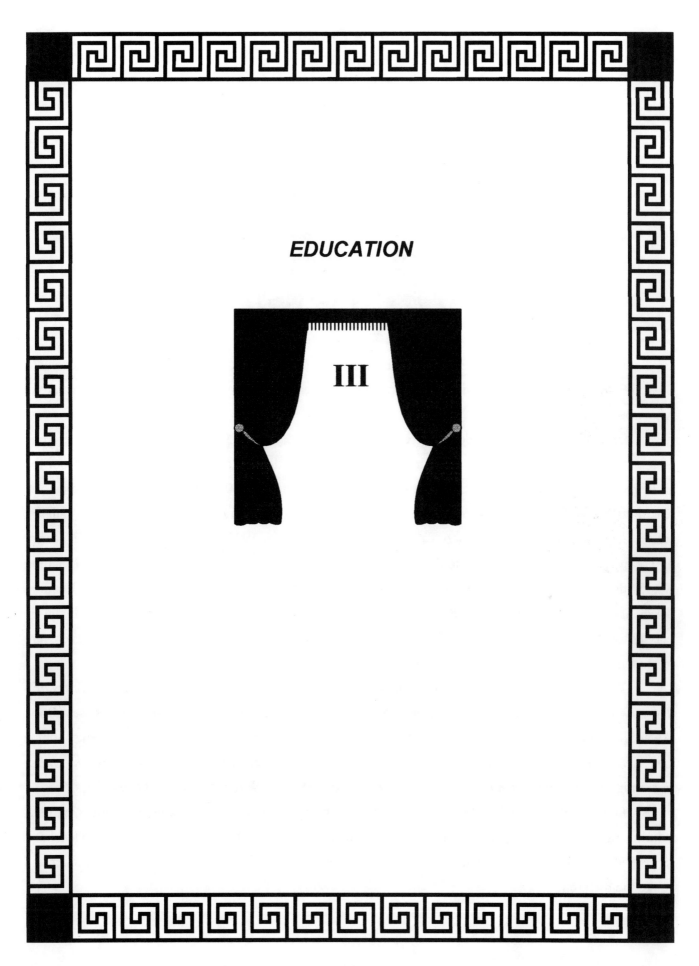

III

Sharon Draper
(1948–)
EDUCATOR

The 1997 National Teacher of the year was born to teach. As a girl growing up in Cleveland, Sharon Draper taught her dolls and the neighborhood children. She enjoyed learning and talked to anyone who would listen.

Draper received her bachelor's degree in 1970 from Pepperdine University and master's in English education from Miami University in Ohio. She was awarded the doctorate of Human Letters from the College of Mount Saint Joseph in Cincinnati. She began teaching in 1970. She landed a premiere position teaching English at the highly respected magnet school, Walnut Hills High in Cincinnati in 1979. Sharon was selected Outstanding High School Language Arts Educator for 1995 and Ohio Teacher of the Year in 1997. In 1996, Draper was elected to the board of directors of the Nation Board for Professional Teaching Standards. She is an active member of the National Council of Teachers of English, International Reading Association, Delta Kappa Gamma, and the Honor Society for Women Educators. Students love Draper's classes for many reasons. She encourages students to ask questions. Her lessons and materials are relevant to students' lives.

When Draper is not teaching or taking courses, she is writing books. Her first book, *Tears of a Tiger*, won the Coretta Scott King Genesis Award and the American Library Association's Best Book Award for young adults. *Forged by Fire* won the Coretta Scott King Award in 1998. Other books include *One Small Torch; Shadows of Caesar's Creek; Ziggy and the Black Dinosaurs; Romiette and Julio; Jazzimagination; The Touch of a Teacher; Let the Circle Be Unbroken;* and *Battered Bones*.

During her reign as Teacher of the Year, Draper traveled the country speaking to teachers, parents, administrators, and policy makers. She works with the Mayerson Academy designed to improve teacher's skills and classroom management. She has four children. Her philosophy is "The touch of a teacher will make the difference."

44

Johnetta Cole
(1936–)
EDUCATOR

Johnetta Cole was born in Jacksonville, Florida, to a prominent family, who owned an insurance company. Her mother taught English at a local college. She entered Fisk at fifteen years of age and studied under Arna Bontemps. In 1953 she transferred to Oberlin College in Ohio to be with her sister. There she studied anthropology and graduated in1957. In 1959 Cole worked and studied in Liberia. Her dissertation was "The Traditional and Wage Earnings Labor in Liberia." She studied under noted anthropologists Melville Herskovitz and Paul Bohannan at Northwestern University in Evanston, Illinois. She received her Ph.D. in 1967.

Cole has had a very distinguished teaching career. She was voted Outstanding Faculty Member of the Year in 1965 at Washington State. In 1970, she helped to develop the African American Studies Department at the University of Massachusetts. She was the director of Latin American Studies and Caribbean Studies at Hunter College in New York from 1983 to 1987. She has also taught at Williams College in Massachusetts and Oberlin College.

While at Hunter, in 1986, she released her landmark book *All-American Woman*. She was an active contributor to *Black Scholar* magazine. Her other books include *Dream the Boldest Dream* and *Straight Talk with America's Sister President*.

History was made in 1987 when Cole became the first African American woman to become president of Spelman College. Under her leadership, she improved the quality of the faculty, enhanced the institution's research department, and enlarged the endowment to $113 million, with Bill and Camille Cosby's generous contribution of $20 million. Spelman has been voted the best college of all colleges in the country by several studies and magazines.

In 1997, Cole resigned from Spelman after 10 years and returned to her first love—the classroom. She is a professor of anthropology at Emory University in Atlanta.

Johnetta Cole has received numerous awards and more than fifteen honorary doctorates. She is married and has three sons.

Marva Collins
(1936–)
EDUCATOR

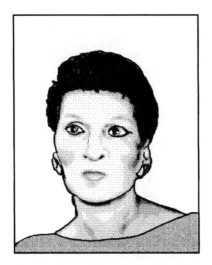

Marva Collins was born in Monroeville, Alabama. She raved about her father, who fought against Jim Crow and became financially stable in spite of discrimination. Collins could read before entering elementary school. Her spirit was challenged in high school, which required all females to take home economics class. Marva had no intention of becoming a domestic, and enrolled in typing because she was going to college. In 1953, she was the only female to graduate from Clark College in Atlanta in secretarial science.

Unfortunately, due to discrimination, she was unable to find work and "resorted" to teaching in Monroeville. After two years, she relocated to Chicago and continued teaching. She loved teaching but took issue with public education's insensitivity to poor people, its low expectations of students, excessive administrative paperwork, and pettiness among staff members.

In 1975, Collins left Chicago Public Schools and formed the Daniel Hale Williams Westside Preparatory School in the basement of a community college. She reserved books from the garbage can of her former school and used them to teach her first four students.

Two decades later, thousands of children have been educated, 30,000 teachers have been retrained by Marva, and she has franchised her school to California, Oklahoma, Cincinnati, Milwaukee, and Kenosha. She has been featured on *60 Minutes,* and a television movie has been made about her. Her philosophy is simple: "I will teach and you will learn." Her son Patrick is the administrator of the Chicago school. Collins has even returned to the Chicago Public Schools as a consultant to improve low achieving schools.

Collins loves to read; she averages almost 500 books a year. She has written *Marva Collins' Way, Ordinary Children, Extra Ordinary Teacher*s, and *Values: Lighting the Candle of Excellence.*

She has received numerous awards and more than forty honorary doctorates. She is married and has two children.

Barbara Sizemore
(1927–)
EDUCATOR

Barbara Sizemore has been involved in the education of African American children all of her adult life. She was born and raised in Chicago and is the product of Chicago Public Schools. She earned her bachelor's (1947) and master's degrees (1954) from Northwestern University. Her doctorate in education administration was from the University of Chicago in 1979. She is also the recipient of four honorary degrees.

Sizemore embarked on her teaching career in 1947. She has taught all grades K–12. Her areas of expertise include Latin, Spanish, and Special Education. Sizemore remained in the classroom for fifteen years before becoming a principal. Over the next decade she was an elementary and high school principal. As a classroom teacher and an administrator, she improved the academic achievement of her students. She demanded excellence of her staff and students.

In 1973, Sizemore became Superintendent of Washington, D.C., public schools. She served in that capacity for three years. Sizemore relocated to Pittsburgh and became a professor at the University of Pittsburgh. She remained in Pittsburgh from 1977 through 1992 and retired professor emerita.

Sizemore returned home to Chicago in 1992 and became Dean of the School of Education at DePaul University. Sizemore founded the School Achievement Structure (SAS) which provides consulting and technical assistance to low-achieving schools. She is the director of the National Association of Black School Educators' research arm, which is the Moody Institute. She is a consultant to more than 100 agencies, colleges, public school systems, and state departments of education. She retired from DePaul in 1998 as professor emerita.

Sizemore continues to consult. She has written hundreds of professional articles. She is the mother of six children and the grandmother of three.

Verta Mae Grosvenor
(1938–)
EDUCATOR

When Verta Mae Grosvenor prepares a meal, one can expect to learn much more than simply how to mix ingredients. Grosvenor's style reflects a rich history of the significance of food to the African American experience and to various cultures throughout the world. There is always a lesson to be learned when Verta Mae Grosvenor is in the kitchen. More than just a chef, Grosvenor is considered to be a "culinary anthropologist."

Grosvenor was born in Fairfax, South Carolina, on April 4, 1938. As the only survivor of premature twins, Grosvenor was thought to be a miracle child. Her delicate health would not allow for picking cotton, so the young girl spent her time learning how to prepare meals for the family. To Grosvenor, the stories and the history she heard over the cooking pot were just as important to the food as the seasonings.

Grosvenor was greatly influenced by strong extended family ties. When she was a teenager, her knowledge of cooking styles expanded when her family moved to Pennsylvania. Grosvenor had been kicked in the head by a mule. Because of the Jim Crow policies of the time, the family was forced to relocate to Philadelphia to seek medical attention. In Philadelphia, Grosvenor was taught the importance of "tribal love," or remaining connected to family, by her namesake, Aunt Verta. Grosvenor's grandmother, Estella, helped Verta Mae Grosvenor to hone her cooking skills and influenced the young woman's unique sense of style. Grosvenor's Aunt Rose from Harlem taught her about "survival cooking." "Survival cooking" referred to a style born of the spirit of courage of the ancestors which allowed them to live the good life in the face of great adversity. One uncle told Grosvenor stories about the food that was prepared for Harriet Tubman and her groups of runaway slaves at stops on the Underground Railroad. Grosvenor's father helped to encourage in Verta Mae an excitement for cooking.

Also a writer, Grosvenor's works include such colorful titles as her autobiographical *Vibration Cooking: or The Traveling Notes of a Geechee Girl* (1976), *Thursdays and Every Other Sunday Off: A Domestic Rap* (1972), and *Plain Brown Rapper* (1975). Her writing assignments have taken her all over the world. Travels to Paris, Brazil, and Cuba as a writer have also served to expand her culinary repertoire. Grosvenor's talents reflect influences from the West Indies to India. Grosvenor's travels have helped her to understand, through food, that the peoples of the world don't live in isolated groups but influence each other through often subtle cultural connections. For Grosvenor, the kitchen is a symbol of the world. Through her talents, she helps to explain how people of African descent have enhanced the flavors of foods on an international level.

She has two daughters.

Asa Hilliard III
(1933–)
EDUCATOR, PSYCHOLOGIST, AND HISTORIAN

Asa Hilliard was born in Galveston, Texas. His grandfather and father were both high school principals. Hilliard earned his bachelor's (1955), master's (1961), and doctor's degrees (1963) at the University of Denver. Hilliard taught in Liberia for six years while on assignment as professor for eighteen years at San Francisco State University. Hilliard can't be pigeonholed into one particular field. His strengths are in education, psychology, and African history.

Hilliard is the current Fuller E. Callaway Professor at Georgia State University in the Department of Education Policy Studies and the Department of Educational Psychology. He has written several books, including *Testing African American Students; The Teaching of Ptah Hotep; SBA: The Reawakening of the African Mind;* and *The Maroon within Us.* He has written hundreds of articles for various journals.

Hilliard researched the discriminatory impact of IQ scores on African American children. As a result, IQ scores cannot be used in California to track children. His research for the National Association of Black School Educators (NABSE) on models of excellence was significant in the development of high-achieving schools. He is a sought-after consultant to thousands of schools nationwide. He has received numerous awards including educator of the year from NABSE and psychologist of the year from the Association of Black Psychologists.

Hilliard is one of the founders of the Association for the Study of Classical African Civilizations (ASCAC). He has produced a powerful Africentric presentation entitled: *Free Your Mind and Return to the Source.* Hilliard provides educational tours to Africa for those interested in visiting the continent and learning more about their roots.

He is married and he and his wife have four children.

Molefi Asante
(1942–)
EDUCATOR AND AUTHOR

Molefi Asante was born in Valdosa, Georgia. Asante was a serious student inspired by his grand-father. He earned his bachelor's degree in 1964 from Oklahoma Christian College. Asante secured his master's degree in 1965 from Pepperdine University. His Ph.D., in African American studies, came from UCLA in 1968. He was the SNCC chapter president while at UCLA. He worked in Zimbabwe and speaks French, German, Spanish, and Kiswahili.

Asante became a professor at the young age of thirty at the State University of New York at Buffalo. He taught there from 1973-1984 and moved to Temple in 1985. He created the first doctoral program in African American Studies in 1987 at Temple. Dr. Asante advocates the evolution of African American Studies into a respected discipline. He also advocates that issues should be viewed from an African frame of reference. African people should be viewed as subjects, not objects, concerning their experiences. This has led to the terminology Afrocentric, Africentric, Afrocentricity and Africentricity.

Asante illustrates his seriousness about the subject with more than forty-five books, including *Afrocentricity; Afrocentric Idea; Kemet, Afrocentricity, and Knowledge; African Intellectual Heritage; African Cultural Atlas;* and *Classical Africa* among others.

He has written more than 200 scholarly articles about the African experience. Asante is the founder and editor of the *Journal of Black Studies*. He frequently provides tours of Africa to interested students and community residents.

Asante is a consultant to numerous school districts that are interested in making their curriculum more Afrocentric. He is the founder of the National Afrocentric Institute.

Molefi Asante is married with three children.

John Henrik Clarke
(1915–1998)
HISTORIAN

John Henrik Clarke was born in Union Springs, Alabama, and had seven siblings. The family moved to Columbus, Georgia. His parents were sharecroppers. John moved to Harlem in 1933. He took courses at Columbia University and received his doctorate in 1978 via correspondence. He read everything related to the history and empowerment of African people. He studied under Arnold Schaumburg and the work of Edward Wilmont Blyden and J. A. Rodgers. His friends included Cheikh Anta Diop, Yosef ben Jochannon, Kwame Nkrumah, and Malcolm X. Dr. Clarke's major belief was that history is a clock that tells where you are and what you must do.

Clarke taught at Hunter College and Cornell University. A library is named after him at the latter school. Clarke was a prolific writer. His books include *Africa Counts*; *African People in World History*; *Africa at the Crossroads*; *Black American Short Stories*; *Malcolm X: The Man and His Times*; *Marcus Garvey and The Vision of Africa*; *Who Betrayed the African: World Revolution*; *Christopher Columbus and the African Holocaust*, and many more. He also edited and contributed numerous articles to collections.

From 1962 to 1882, Clarke served as editor of *Freedomways* magazine. He was a frequent contributor to *Black Scholar* magazine. He was the founder of the African Heritage Studies Association (AHSA) and was active in the African Study of Classical African Civilizations (ASCAC). Many of those members were students of Clarke, and he mentored the organization. Wesley Snipes acted in and was actively involved in the production of *Great and Mighty Walk*, which portrayed the life of Clarke.

Clarke began to lose his sight during the last decade of his life, but he continued to read the literature through braille. He remained active on the speaking circuit up to the last month of his life. Hundreds of people gathered in New York for his funeral. Many cities had their own memorial service for this great historian. He was married with four children.

51

Yosef Ben-Jochannan
(1918–)
HISTORIAN

Dr. Ben, as he is warmly called by his students, admirers, and peers, was born in Ethiopia. His parents traveled extensively throughout Central and South America. Jochannan spent his childhood between South America, Puerto Rico, and Cuba. His interest in history was stimulated at an early age, when an eighth-grade teacher told him that "Negroes have no history." He received his college degrees from the University of Havana in Cuba, the University of Puerto Rico, and the University of Madrid.

Jochannan is the former chairman of the Harlem Preperatory school. He has been a professor in South America, Al Azar University in Cairo, Egypt, Columbia, Rutgers, Cornell, State University of New York at New Paltz, Marymount, Malcolm-King, and Pace College.

He has written numerous books, including *African Origins of Major Western Religions; We the Black Jews; From African Captives to Insane Slaves; A Chronology of the Bible; Axioms and Quotations of Yosef Ben Jochannan; Abu Simbel to Ghizeh; Africa: Mother of Western Civilization; Black Man of the Nile and His Family; Cultural Genocide in the Black and African Studies Curriculum,* and many more.

Dr. Ben is a highly sought after speaker. He is a historian specializing in Egyptology. He refuses to believe civilization started in Greece; nor does he believe that Greeks developed Egypt. He and his colleagues Cheikh Anta Diop, John Henrik Clarke, John Jackson, J. A. Rogers, and numerous others, have fought intellectually for the respect of African history.

He has taken thousands of Africans back to Egypt to document and lecture on the great achievements of Africans before the European invasion. Jochannon has been an advisor to the United Nations Educational, Scientific, and Cultural Organization (UNESCO) and to the government of Zanzibar.

Dr. Ben is married, with twelve biological children, eight adopted children, forty-seven grandchildren, and thirteen great-grandchildren.

Cheikh Anta Diop
(1923–1986)
HISTORIAN

Cheikh Anta Diop was born in Senegal. He developed an expertise in many areas. He was an Egyptologist, linguist, anthropologist, scientist, historian, and writer. His major objective was to prove that ancient Egyptians were descendants of Black Africans, that ancient Egypt was a Black society, and that their cultural achievements predate the influence of Greece and Rome.

Diop developed his various disciplines because he wanted to prove his position in a myriad of ways. He encountered his first obstacle while securing his doctorate from the University of Paris. His dissertation documented the cultural unity of Egypt with other African countries. The university denied his degree in 1954 and did not acquiesce until 1960, when Diop and a team of anthropologists, sociologists, and historians supported his findings. Diop was a professor of Egyptology at the University of Dakar, in Senegal from 1961 until his death.

Diop showed the linguistic similarities in the vocabularies of Egyptians and Africans in the south. As an anthropologist, Diop documented that the first human was identified in Southeast Africa, almost five million years ago. As a scientist, he supported the above with the carbon 14 dating procedure. As a historian, he said Egyptians had black skin and kinky hair.

As a writer and educator, he expressed these ideas in *Cultural Unity of Black Africa; African Origin of Civilization; Civilization or Barbarism;* and *Precolonial Black Africa: A Comparative Study of the Political and Social Systems of Europe and Black Africa.*

Diop was very much aware of the war in academia over Egypt. People who believe in White supremacy are not going to accept that Black Africans developed Ancient Egypt. They will continue to espouse that Rome and Greece shared in the building of this great civilization. Diop has inspired many African historians, anthropologists, and scholars to continue this fight.

BUSINESS, PUBLISHING AND PRODUCTION

IV

Reginald Lewis
(1942–1993)
ENTREPRENEUR

A poor Black paperboy became the wealthiest Black man in America, worth more than $400 million. At his funeral, Bill Cosby said that his friend, Reggie Lewis, played the hell out of his hand.

Reggie Lewis was born in Baltimore, Maryland. He was a very good student and a quarterback on his high school team. He earned a bachelor's degree from Virginia State University in 1965 and completed his law degree at Harvard's Law School in 1968.

Lewis encountered many experiences of racial discrimination in the corporate sector. He could have reduced these skirmishes if he had confined himself exclusively to the Black business sector. The beauty of Reggie was that he could not be confined. His autobiography, *Why Should White Guys Have All the Fun?*, appropriately described Reggie's spirit. He did want to have the largest Black business. He wanted to own the largest business in the world.

He mastered the concept of OPM (Other People's Money) and acquired businesses and sold them, using the proceeds as leverage and collateral for the next purchase. He believed that a global vision plus hard work would allow him to become successful and reduce the ramifications of racism. Often he would work 16 to 20 hours. This unfortunately contributed to the impairment of his health.

In three successive acquisitions, Lewis secured a business for $22, $90, and $985 million. The last acquisition, the purchase of Beatrice Foods, was his shining moment. It was a Fortune 100 company with global operations. The purchase was the talk of Wall Street and Black Enterprise. Everyone wanted to understand how a Black man had become so successful.

Lewis was very generous in supporting his two alma maters as well as Howard University. The International Law School at Harvard is named after him. He became the only African American to have a building named in his honor.

He is survived by his wife and two daughters. The family continues to operate the business.

Robert Johnson
(1947–)
ENTREPRENEUR

Robert Johnson was one of nine children born in Hickory, Mississippi. The family moved to Freeport, Illinois. Robert was a very good student. He earned a bachelor's degree from the University of Illinois and a master's degree from Princeton's Woodrow Wilson School of Public Policy. He became the press secretary for Washington, D.C. Congressman Walter Fauntroy. He moved on to become vice president for National Cable company of government relations, which is responsible for monitoring national cable companies.

Johnson had a dream of owning a cable company. In 1980, he made his dream a reality with the formation of Black Entertainment Television (BET). They first aired musical videos and reruns of Black sit-coms. The response was overwhelming. Johnson has expanded the format to include news, talk shows, sports events, movies, and pay-per view. BET features rap, jazz, R&B, and gospel music videos.

BET now reaches more than 55 million households, with advertising revenue in excess of $200 million. BET employees 600 people. Johnson also publishes three magazines: *Emerge, BET Weekend,* and *Heart and Soul.* He also acquired Arabesque Books, which specializes in romantic fiction. His objective is to develop a movie studio to produce these romance novels. BET owns a restaurant in Washington, D.C.

He has collaborated with Microsoft to expand into the Internet and software. Johnson partnered with Chase Bank to produce a credit card and other financial services. Johnson partnered with Disney to produce a Black theme park in Orlando. He also envisions a clothing line and a casino hotel in Las Vegas.

Johnson is on the boards of several major companies. The boy from Hickory, who had a dream now lives in a $4.3 million estate on 133 acres in Virginia with his wife and two children.

Berry Gordy
(1929–)
ENTREPRENEUR

Berry Gordy was born in Detroit, the seventh of eight children. He dropped out of high school to become a boxer, when that failed, Gordy entered the army and earned his GED. Upon completion of duty, he opened a record store. Unfortunately, this venture failed. He began working on the Ford assembly line and writing music.

In 1957, Gordy met Jackie Wilson and felt there was a perfect marriage between his songs and Wilson's majestic voice. They produced four songs. Their big hit was "Reet Petite." The song, "To be Loved" became the title of his autobiography three decades later.

Gordy's greatest gift is his judge of talent. He met Smokey Robinson in 1957 and recognized not only his beautiful voice, but his tremendous writing ability. Later, when he was introduced to the Holland brothers, he again acknowledged their great writing ability.

On January 12, 1959, his family lent him $800.00 to start Motown Records. Their first building which was actually a house was called Hitsville USA. One of the rooms was called Studio A. Some of the greatest songs of all time were produced in Studio A. Gordy was very cognizant that the strength of Motown was based on their ability to write and produce good music.

His next goal was to secure the best singing talent in Black America. Gordy met the Matadors and turned them into Miracles. He was introduced to the Primettes and converted them into Supremes. He heard the Distants and molded them into Temptations. Along the way, Gordy signed Mary Wells, Martha and the Vandellas, The Marvelettes, Gladys Knight and the Pips, the Four Tops, Marvin Gaye, Stevie Wonder and many more. Can you imagine music without these giants?

Their first number 1 record was "Please Mr. Postman" by the Marvelettes in 1961. In 1969, Gordy signed the Jacksons. Michael became an instant star and Motown continued to soar. Artists positively competed with each other for stardom. In 1970, six of fourteen top ten releases went number one. The Supremes ranked fourth in total record sales after Michael Jackson, The Beatles, and Elvis Presley.

In 1972, Gordy relocated Motown to Los Angeles. He wanted the company to produce motion pictures. His films included *Bingo Long, Lady Sings the Blues, Mahogany,* and *The Wiz.* There were many television specials including Motown 25.

In 1977, Motown had the largest sales of any African American company. Gordy had leveraged $800 into a company that had annual sales of almost $500 million in 18 years.

There were many challenges in the expansion. Many groups wanted their own writers and more money. Other record companies successfully robbed Motown's talent. Many felt the move to Los Angeles thwarted the tremendous talent coming out of Detroit. Others felt the Mafia made distribution more problematic and forced Gordy to sell.

In 1988, Gordy sold Motown for $61 million to Boston Ventures. Amazingly, a few years later it was sold to Polygram for $301 million.

Gordy has four children and one of his labels was named after three of them JoBet, in honor of Joy, Berry, and Terry.

Kenneth Chenault

(1952–)

BUSINESS EXECUTIVE

Kenneth Chenault was born and raised in Hempstead, New York. He learned humility from his father. As a child, he was looking through some of his father's papers and saw that his father had scored the highest on his dental board exam. When he queried his father, all he said was, "We all have a responsibility to be the best." That lesson stayed with his son.

Chenault was an excellent student and earned a bachelor's degree in history from Bowdoin College. He earned his law degree from Harvard. After law school he worked with a law firm for two years.

In 1981, he was noticed by recruiters at American Express. His first assignment was in the strategic planning division. He remained there for eight years and became the director of the division. In 1989, Chenault became president of the Consumer Card Group. There were major challenges in this department, including stiff competition from other card companies. Before he left in 1993, he made the division profitable and improved market share.

American Express showed their supreme confidence in Kenneth when he became President of Travel Related Services, which is the most profitable division of the company. The media realized that Chenault could rise to the top of this Fortune 500 company. He was featured in magazines and newspapers and received numerous awards. Chenault took all this in the same stride as his father took his dental exam scores.

In 1995, Chenault was named vice chairman of American Express, placing him second only to the chairman. When the chairman retires in 2004, Chenault will become the first African American chairman and CEO of a Fortune 500 company. Chenault serves on the boards of many corporations.

Ken is married with three children.

T. Thomas Fortune
(1856–1928)
PUBLISHER

Timothy Thomas Fortune was born in October 1856 to slave parents in Marianna, Florida, with Black, Native American, and Irish blood flowing through his veins. His family's political activities forced them to flee to Jacksonville, Florida, where he had a limited education through the Freedmen's Bureau. Fortune learned the printer's trade and became an expert in composition.

In 1876, he briefly attended Howard University in Washington, D.C., and began his love affair with journalism while working on the Black newspaper *People's Advocate*. Soon after, he met and married Carrie C. Smiley, and later he returned with her to his native Florida.

In the late 1870s, Fortune moved to New York City, getting a job first as a printer and then almost immediately as part owner of the weekly tabloid *Rumor*. He later became editor of the newspaper and changed the name to Globe. Shortly afterward, he became sole owner of his first newspaper, the *New York Freeman*, which later became *New York Age*. Fortune believed the paper's purpose was to counter negative coverage of Blacks by the White press. Fortune's editorial policies advocated Black self-reliance, demanded full equality for African Americans, and condemned all forms of discrimination.

In the mid-1880s, two general circulation papers, the *Boston Transcript* and the New York Sun, hired Fortune as a reporter and editor, which was unusual for a Black man in those days. He traveled frequently, reporting on the conditions of the South. Fortune was an early advocate of the term Afro-American. He considered Negro to be a term of contempt.

Fortune wrote three books: *Black and White: Land and Politics in the South* (1884), a historical essay on land, labor, and politics in the South which called for the unification of workers of both races; *The Negro in Politics*, published in 1885; and *Dreams of Life*, published in 1905.

Fortune later founded the National Afro-American League, which unfortunately was shortlived. The organization pioneered many programs and methods used by many modern-day civil rights groups. In 1898, he formed the National Afro-American Council. The council held conferences emphasizing civil rights, women's suffrage, and concern over the fate of Latin Americans after the United States defeated Spain. Unfortunately, political in fighting over his support of Black leader Booker T. Washington severely weakened the organization. The legacies of Fortune's groups helped set the platform for the NAACP, which was organized formally in 1910, and influenced its ongoing fight to end discrimination in all forms.

In the early 1900s, Fortune suffered from a bout of mental illness, possibly due to alcoholism, and for several years he was virtually a derelict. When his health returned, he returned to writing fiery editorials for Marcus Garvey's *Negro World*.

Timothy Thomas Fortune died in 1928 in Philadelphia, Pennsylvania.

Earl G. Graves

(1935–)

PUBLISHER AND ENTREPRENEUR

The son of a shipping clerk, Earl Gilbert Graves was born in Brooklyn, New York, in 1935. Graves went on to attend Morgan State College, where he received a bachelor's degree in economics in 1958. During the early 1960s, Graves tried his hand at real estate. He also served as national commissioner of Scouting for the Boy Scouts of America. Graves got a taste of politics when he worked as an administrative assistant for the late Senator Robert Kennedy in 1965. Always up for a challenge, Graves left the political arena and started a management consulting firm in 1968.

Referred to by Jesse Jackson, Sr., as the "primary educator in the country on trends and opportunities in Black business," Earl G. Graves has long been a force to be reckoned within Black corporate America. As founder and publisher of *Black Enterprise* magazine, he has an inside understanding of the past and present dynamics of Black-owned businesses in the United States that few professionals possess.

In 1970, Graves left the firm and embarked on the endeavor for which he is best known—a magazine which would effectively gauge and explain trends influencing the development of Black business in America. In this year *Black Enterprise* magazine was born. Today, almost thirty years old, *Black Enterprise* has a readership of over a quarter of a million people and annual revenues of more than $15 million.

Graves tried his hand at yet another venture in 1990. He bought the rights for the Washington, D.C., Pepsi Cola distribution operations with his partner, basketball star Earvin "Magic" Johnson. As chief executive officer, Graves lent his Midas touch to yet another enterprise. With a distribution of more than four million cases of Pepsi annually, the franchise is worth an estimated $60 million.

As the twenty-first century approaches, Graves stresses the importance of bridging the gap between the net worth of the average Black family and the average White family. He has also been a strong advocate of mainstream Black involvement in the financial realm—not only through ownership and entrepreneurship but also through investment and a basic understanding of the stock market. Graves has written an advice manual for Black professionals with the attention-grabbing title *How to Succeed in Business without Being White*.

Earl is married and has three sons who are active in the business.

RELIGION

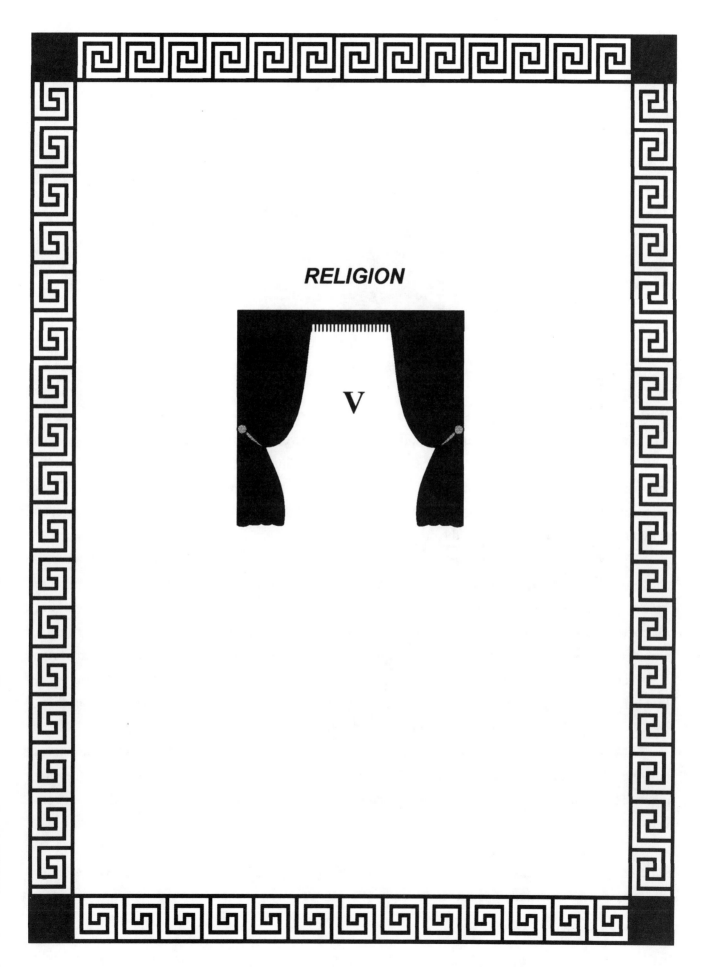

V

Dr. Gardner Taylor
(1918–)

MINISTER

He was born in Baton Rouge, Louisiana. Gardner confessed Christ as Lord of his life at an early age. Taylor earned his bachelor's degree at Leland College in 1937 and a doctorate in ministry from Oberlin University.

His first pastorate was Bethany Baptist in Ohio, followed by Beaulah, and Mt. Zion in Louisiana. In 1948, he became the pastor of the great Concord Baptist Church in Brooklyn, New York. Under his leadership of 42 years, the congregation grew from 1,000 to more than 10,000 members. Dr. Taylor created an elementary school, nursing home, credit union, senior citizen housing, clothing exchange, and many other ministries to empower the community.

The entire nation saw the many gifts in this talented preacher. Dr. Taylor was asked to eulogize many great people in the Black community, including Dr. Martin Luther King, Jr. and Dr. Samuel Proctor. Time magazine called him the "Dean of Black Preachers." Ebony magazine ranked him the greatest Black preacher in America. People leave his sermon which normally does exceed 30 minutes clamoring for more. Gardner is considered one of the most humble men in America who makes everyone feel important.

He has written several books including, *The Certain Sound of the Trumpet: Crafting a Sermon of Authority; We Have This Ministry: The Heart of the Pastor's Vocation; Chariots Aflame; How Shall They Preach;* and *The Scarlet Thread: Nineteen Sermons.*

Many seminaries use his books and tapes in their curricula. He has been a guest lecturer at many of them including Union, Harvard, Yale, and Princeton. Duke University has named a series of lectures in his honor. He has received numerous honorary doctorates and awards. He has preached on all seven continents.

Dr. Taylor retired from Concord in 1990 and became Pastor Emeritus. The street adjacent to the church is named in his honor. Churches nationwide continue to seek him for his great preaching.

Gardner is married with one daughter.

Jeremiah A. Wright, Jr.
(1941–)
MINISTER

Ironically, Rev. Wright almost died at birth from complications. He was born in rural Virginia and raised in Philadelphia. His parents are both ministers and each has a doctorate. Wright earned a bachelor's degree from Howard University in 1968 and two-master's degrees—one from Howard University (1969) and the other from the University of Chicago (1975). He earned his doctorate from United Theological Seminary in 1990. His four books include *What Makes You So Strong?; Africans Who Shaped Our Faith; Good News For Black Families;* and *When Black Men Stand Up for God: Reflections on the Million Man March.* He is one of the most sought after preachers in this country.

Jeremiah A. Wright, Jr., speaks more than five languages, has earned four degrees, plays keyboard, sings, preaches revivals during the week, preaches three sermons at his home church on Sunday, and has grown a church from 87 members in 1972 to more than 7,000 today.

Rev. Wright's love for the Lord is best expressed in his pastorate of Trinity United Church of Christ in Chicago. He became the pastor in 1972 when the church had 87 members. He had a ten-point plan: a worshiping, spirit-filled, praying, tithing, Bible-based, progressive, politically aware, loving, working, community-conscious church. Twenty-seven years later, the church has more than 7,000 members and 80 ministries, 25 percent of which is geared toward youth. Women have leadership positions, including ministers and deacons. Men and youth are encouraged and made to feel important.

Wright's sermons are filled with scripture, historical and contemporary analysis, appreciation of Black history, humor, and unconditional love of Jesus Christ.

He is married with five children and two grandchildren.

Samuel DeWitt Proctor
(1921–1997)

MINISTER AND EDUCATOR

Samuel DeWitt Proctor was born in Norfolk, Virginia, to God-fearing parents who valued education. He had five siblings. Proctor was a brilliant student. He skipped three grades in high school. He earned his bachelor's degree at Virginia Union (1942), his master's degree at Crozier (1945), and his doctorate in Ministry from Boston University in 1950. Proctor did postgraduate work in Social Ethics at Yale University.

Proctor pastored his first church, Pond Street Baptist Church, at the age of twenty-four while studying at Yale. He encouraged many Northern youth to attend Black colleges in the South.

He returned to his alma mater, Virginia Union, as president in 1950, the youngest ever at the ripe age of twenty-nine. He demanded excellence of his students and inspired them to reach their full potential. Later he assumed leadership of North Carolina A&T for two terms as president. One of his students, whom he mentored, was Jesse Jackson, Sr. Proctor served as associate director of the Peace Corps under Presidents Kennedy and Johnson. This responsibility required living part of the time in Nigeria.

He inspired Martin Luther King, Jr., to attend Crozier and was available to him for advice. He also reached out to congressman and pastor Adam Clayton Powell. When Powell died, Abyssinia recruited Proctor in 1971 to serve as their pastor. Proctor was a great preacher, teacher, and administrator. He groomed Calvin Butts as his assistant pastor. After seventeen years, he passed the baton to his protégé. He was pastor emeritus at Abyssinia.

While pastoring Abyssinia and afterwards, Proctor returned to his first love—the classroom. He taught at the University of Wisconsin, Yale, United Theological, Duke, Vanderbilt, and finally Rutgers, where he retired as professor emeritus.

Proctor found time to write *Substance of Things Hoped For; The Certain Sound of the Trumpet: Crafting a Sermon of Authority; My Moral Odyssey;* and *How Shall They Hear: Effective Preaching for Vital Faith.*

The greatest legacy Proctor left are the thousands of men and women who benefitted from the great man's wisdom and vast experience.

Proctor is survived by a wife and four sons.

Father Divine
(1877–1965)
MINISTER

Father Divine was born George Baker in Savannah, Georgia. Father Divine was a Black American who rose to prominence as a religious leader. In 1919, he founded the Peace Mission movement. A predominantly Black religious cult in the United States. The Mission worked to end poverty, racial discrimination, and war. His followers worshipped him. They called him God, Dean of the Universe, and Harnesser of Atomic Energy.

In 1915, he started his first church in New York City and took the name Major J. Devine. His followers, known as "angels," were encouraged to live together in houses called "heavens," and to contribute their income to the Peace Mission movement. The transition from George Baker to Major J. Devine to Father Divine was essentially completed when he set up his first "heaven" or communal dwelling in Long Island, New York, in 1919. Legal entanglements forced him to relocate to Manhattan (Harlem). But the cult continued to grow and spread throughout the many cities of the northern and western United States. The organization expanded rapidly during the 1930s and 1940s.

He preached total racial integration and did not permit his followers to smoke, drink liquor, or use cosmetics. Father Divine supported Black businesses. During the Great Depression, grocery stores and other businesses owned by the movement provided food, clothing, and other goods to the poor, at little or no cost.

Father Divine led a luxurious lifestyle and was often criticized for it. But his goals, spiritual leadership, and generosity attracted supporters in cities throughout the United States. The key to Father Divine's success was the devotion of competent disciples. On October 10, 1965, Father Divine passed away. After his death, interest in the movement declined sharply.

Elijah Muhammad

(1897–1975)

MINISTER

Elijah Muhammad was born Elijah Poole on October 10, 1897, in Sandersville, Georgia. Muhammad was one of thirteen children born of former slaves. A major turning point occurred in his life when, as a young child, he witnessed the lynching of a Black man by three Whites. This event may have triggered his ultimate belief that Blacks and Whites should live separately and independently.

In 1923, he moved to Detroit. During the 1930s, he became a follower of Wallace Fard. Fard preached that by practicing their "original" religion, Islam, Blacks could overcome degradation in America. Fard encouraged him to reject his "slave" name and adopt an Islamic one. Thus, Elijah Poole became Elijah Muhammad. Fard then appointed him the supreme minister of the Nation of Islam or the Black Muslims. In 1934, Fard disappeared, and Muhammad preached that Fard had actually been Allah in disguise, who shared secrets and teachings with him. This made him "The Messenger of Allah," and he soon began traveling the country, spreading the teachings of the Muslim movement.

That same year, Muhammad was arrested for not sending his children to public school (they attended a Nation of Islam school), and he lived as a fugitive from 1934 to 1942. In 1942, he was arrested again, this time for resisting the draft. Upon his release four years later, he continued his reign as the influential head of the Nation of Islam. In 1950, Muhammad recruited Malcolm X to be the national spokesman for the Nation. Malcolm spent thirteen years in that position, making them the most fruitful years the organization had ever known.

Muhammad and the Nation of Islam earned great respect because of their course of action in the Black community. The group possessed strong self-respect, morals, and values. They did not drink, smoke, gamble, or do drugs. Always self-disciplined and courteous, the group always maintained intact family units.

Muhammad used his followers to show Black America that they could reach the same level of dignity as Whites, and they could do it without their assistance. He believed in separatism and was able to create, with the assistance of his followers and the organization, many alternative institutions. By 1975, the Nation of Islam controlled a vast empire estimated at $80 to $100 million. The group's assets included schools, numerous farms and small businesses, a publishing company, an airplane, an import business, orchard, dairy, refrigerator trucks, apartment complexes, several mansions, and hundreds of houses of worship.

Muhammad was the head of the Nation of Islam for 41 years and lead the spreading of Islam throughout Black America. His self-help movement empowered Blacks to control and determine their own destinies. On February 25, 1975, Elijah Muhammad died of congestive heart failure brought on by lifelong bronchial problems.

Louis Farrakhan
(1933–)
MINISTER

Minister Louis Farrakhan was born Louis Eugene Walcott in New York. In the 1950s, he attended Winston-Salem Teachers College. Later, he moved to Boston and studied violin and guitar. Farrakhan was a superb performer. His stage name was Calypso Gene and he sang Caribbean music. His talents caught the eye of his soon-to-be-mentor, Malcolm X, who recruited him into the Nation of Islam in 1955.

Farrakhan grew very close to Minister Elijah Muhammad. Farrakhan will always be associated with Malcolm X's assassination in 1964. Farrakhan had chosen to follow his teacher rather than his mentor.

Unfortunately, Minister Muhammad died in 1975, and the Nation of Islam was in a shambles. There were squabbles over leadership, direction, and financial solvency. Warith Deen Muhammad, the son of Minister Muhammad, decided to eliminate Black nationalism from the Nation and liquidate the businesses that were considered marginal.

This infuriated Farrakhan, and he set out on a mission in 1975 to rebuild the Nation. Two decades later, they have mosques in 120 cities. Their newspaper, The *Final Call,* has gone weekly, with a circulation of 500,000. They have several restaurants nationwide. They have utilized their strong male population to garner security contracts. Farrakhan negotiated with President Qudafi of Libya to receive a $5 million interest-free loan to produce cosmetic products.

Farrakhan is a gifted speaker and probably can outdraw any speaker in the country. In 1995 he spearheaded the highly successful Million Man March. He desires to duplicate the effort with a Million Families March in 2000. He is married and has nine children.

Johnnie Coleman
MINISTER

Johnnie Coleman was born in Centerville, Alabama. She struggled with low self-esteem due to dark skin, being tall, and her relationship with her father. He wanted a son and named her Johnnie. She was denied admission into a Black sorority because of her darker hue. Coleman graduated from Wiley College in Marshall, Texas in 1943, and later returned in 1977 to earn her doctor of divinity degree.

Her professional career began as a teacher in Canton, Mississippi. Coleman later moved to Chicago and continued teaching. Unfortunately, she was struck with an incurable illness, and she sought spiritual healing. Although raised as a Methodist, Coleman turned to New Thought philosophy taught by Unity headquarters in Lee's Summit, Missouri.

Although Unity believed in New Thought, it still succumbed to racism and discrimination. African Americans could not eat or live in Unity village. Blacks could attend church, but they had to sit in a special roped off section. Coleman was considered arrogant because she fought this discrimination, just as Richard Allen and Absalom Jones had done two centuries prior. Coleman was the first African American to live in the village, although she was set apart from White students.

Coleman graduated in 1956 and became an ordained Unity minister. She founded Christ Unity Center in a YWCA building in Chicago. She became the first African American president of the Association of Unity Churches in 1968. Her church grew and they moved to a facility with a seating capacity of 1,000. She conducted multiple services to accommodate her growing congregation. Coleman withdrew her church from the association due to changes in the by-laws and renamed the congregation Christ Universal Temple (CUT). She also created the Universal Foundation for Better Living. This association boasts a membership of more than 20 similar churches throughout the world. She also founded Johnnie Coleman Institute Bible classes, training programs, and a school for ministers.

In 1985, Coleman built a facility that seats 4,000 people that sit on thirty-two acres of land. The estate includes a restaurant, bookstore, and numerous classrooms. Her future plans include a prayer tower, dormitory, elementary school, performing arts center, and fitness center. It is the largest New Thought church in the country with 25,000 members. CUT has the largest congregation pastored by a woman in the country.

She has been widowed twice but her incurable disease has been removed by her strong faith in God.

T. D. Jakes

(1957–)

MINISTER

T. D. Jakes was born in West Virginia and worked in a local factory, married Serita, and raised five children. He had been nursing a passion to preach God's Word since the age of seventeen. He founded Greater Temple of Faith with ten members and the church grew to more than 1,000 people. One of his major concerns is refuting the belief that Sunday at 11:00 a.m. is the most segregated hour. His vision was an integrated church. In West Virginia, he was able to secure a 40 percent Caucasian congregation.

T. D. Jakes is a powerful preacher. He is able to create an image to the listener while preaching. He is sought all over the country and was chosen to be a bishop by the Full Gospel movement. Jakes saw a need to provide healing sessions exclusively for men, women, and singles. Annually he conducts these three revivals. The response has been astronomical, and he has had to secure coliseums to accommodate crowds that exceed 50,000 people. He has written eighteen books, including two best-sellers, *Woman Thou Art Loosed* and *The Lady, Her Lover, and Her Lord*. Both have sold in excess of one million copies.

The demanding travel schedule and the need to expand brought him to Dallas and the Potter's House church in 1996. The church has grown to 20,000 members, of all races and has acquired 231 acres of land. The area is called a City of Refuge, and ministries will address drug addiction, low self-esteem, employment, wife abuse, parenting, and much more.

LITERATURE AND MEDIA

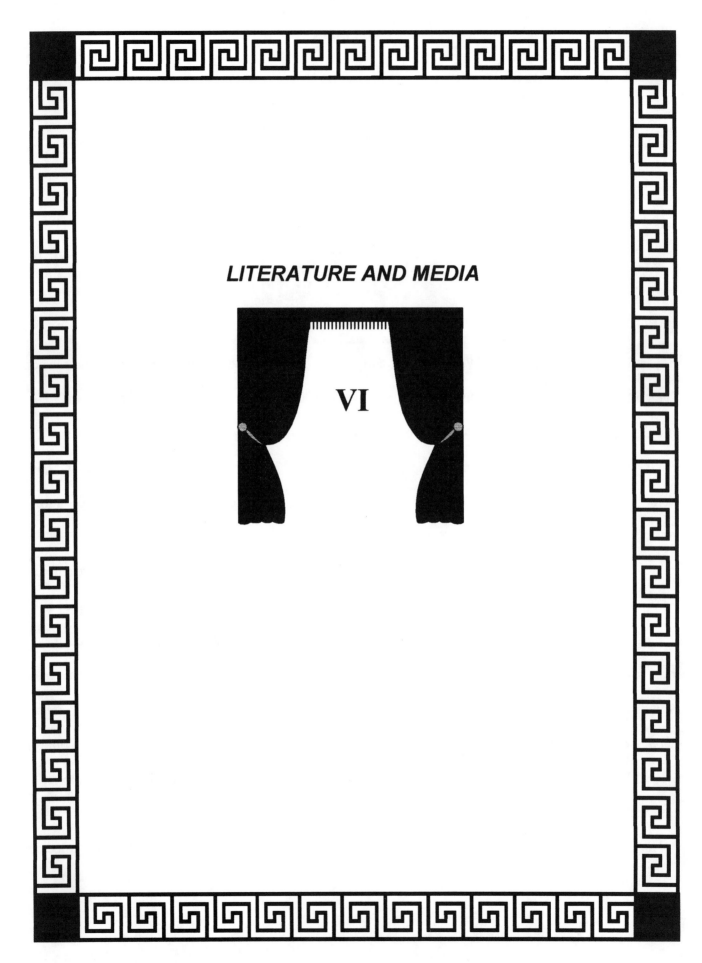

VI

Chinua Achebe

(1930–)

AUTHOR

Chinua Achebe was born in the large village of Ogidi which is one of the first centers of Anglican missionary work in Eastern Nigeria. His father, Isaiah Achebe, was a member of the Church Missionary Society. Achebe studied at Umuahia College and the University College at Ibadan, where he was a medical student, but then switched to English literature. While still in school, he published four articles in the *University Herald.* After graduating in 1953, he went on to work for the Nigerian Broadcasting Corporation as a producer of radio "talks." In 1956 he went to London for a course at the British Broadcasting Corporation. Two years later, while still in London, he published his first novel, *Things Fall Apart.*

After his return to Nigeria, Achebe was appointed Controller of the Eastern Region Station of the Nigerian Broadcasting Corporation. In 1960, the year of Nigerian independence from Britain, he completed his second novel, *No Longer at Ease.*

For the next few years, Achebe traveled widely in East Africa, the United States, Latin American, and Britain. In 1964 he published *Arrow of God.* Achebe's early career in radio ended abruptly in 1966. He left his post as Director of External Broadcasting in Nigeria during the upheaval that led to the Biafran War. He was appointed Senior Research Fellow at the University of Nigeria, Nsukka, and began lecturing widely abroad. That same year he published his fourth book, A Man of the People. He was active on behalf of Biafra, the region of Nigeria that seceded from the Nigerian Federation in 1967.

During the next two decades, Achebe published a political polemic entitled *The Trouble with Nigeria;* a volume of poetry, *Beware of Soul Brother,* which won the Commonwealth Poetry Prize in 1972; and a collection of short stories entitled *Girls at War.* He also gave a number of important talks at conferences in his period, some of which are collected in *Morning Yet on Creation Day.*

During this time, Achebe also undertook a career as a university academic. Along with a fellowship at Nsukka, in 1972 to 1976, and again in 1987 to 1988, he was appointed a professor of English at the University of Massachusetts at Amherst, and also for one year at the University of Connecticut at Storrs. In 1987, he published his fifth novel, *Anthills of the Savannah.* His latest works include *No Longer At Ease, Conversations with Achebe,* and his autobiography.

Achebe has received numerous honors from around the world, including the Honorary Fellowship of the American academy and Institute of Arts and Letters, as well as more than twenty honorary doctorates from universities in England, Scotland, the United States, Canada, and Nigeria. He is also the recipient of Nigeria's highest award for intellectual achievement, the Nigerian National Merit Award. Achebe has been an important force in the development of African writing in his role as the first editor of the Heinemann African Writers.

Currently, Achebe and his wife live in Annandale, New York, where they both teach at Bard College. They have four children.

Terry McMillan
(1951–)
AUTHOR

Terry McMillan was born in Port Huron, Michigan. She has five siblings, including Rosalyn, who has also become a bestselling author. Terry earned a bachelor's degree from the University of California-Berkeley and a master's degree in film from Columbia both in 1979.

She became a tenured Associate Professor at the University of Arizona in 1988. McMillan felt unfulfilled in the classroom and decided to pursue her dream of becoming a writer. Her first book, *Mama,* was released in 1987. Terry realized that a book by an unknown author with little publisher support, she would have to actively promote her own book. She corresponded with Black bookstores and promoted her appearances in the stores. The book enjoyed moderate success and her publisher encouraged her to write another.

McMillan's second book, *Disappearing Acts* (1989), sold almost two million copies. She had struck a nerve among the reading public, especially Black female fiction readers who wanted to better understand relationships. In 1990, she edited an anthology of writers, *Breaking Ice.*

In 1992, McMillan released *Waiting to Exhale.* The book sold more than four million copies and Hollywood loved it enough to produce a movie, which was very successful at the box office. *Waiting to Exhale* described the lives of four women who, though successful in their careers, experience major challenges in their relationships.

McMillan traveled to Jamaica and met a younger man whom she ultimately married. This adventure inspired the book and movie *How Stella Got Her Groove Back* (1996). While not as successful as *Waiting to Exhale*, the book and movie did reasonably well financially.

McMillan's latest book is *A Day Late and a Dollar Short.* They have one son.

Iyanla Vanzant

(1953–)

AUTHOR AND MOTIVATIONAL SPEAKER

Vanzant was born in New York City. She was an unwed teenage mother and the wife of an abusive husband, and at one point seriously contemplated suicide.

Vanzant gave her life to God, left her abusive husband, and raised her three children. She graduated summa cum laude from Medgar Evers College in 1983, and earned her law degree from Queens College in New York in 1988. She passed the bar in Philadelphia and became a public defender. Sister Vanzant is a dynamic motivational speaker and Yoruba priestess.

Iyanla (pronounced Ee Yan-La) Vanzant is the author of the best-selling *Acts of Faith; In the Meantime; One Day My Soul Just Opened Up; The Value in the Valley; Faith in the Valle; Tapping the Power Within; Interiors: A Black Woman's Healing; The Spirit of a Man: A Vision of the Transformation for Black Men and the Women Who Love Them;* and *Yesterday I Cried: Celebrating the Lessons of Living and Loving.*

In her desire to empower people, she realized the legal profession was responding to the problem. Vanzant decided to be proactive and empower people, primarily women, before they reach rock bottom. The purpose of her books and speeches is to help people enhance their self-esteem. She says, "My greatest desire is for people to know who they are from the inside out and to use that knowledge as a tool of empowerment and love." To further her work, Vanzant founded the Inner Visions Spiritual Life Maintenance Network. Her ideas are featured on Hallmark's cards.

The mother of three and grandmother of four, Vanzant lives in Maryland with her longtime friend who is now her husband.

August Wilson
(1945–)
PLAYWRITER

August Wilson was born in Pittsburgh, Pennsylvania. He began his writing career in grade school. After realizing that many of his classmates had forgotten about their heritage, the young writer started putting his feelings and concerns down on paper. In ninth grade he dropped out of school after a teacher accused him of plagiarism; she felt that his work was too good to have been written by a Black person. He continued his education independently through extensive reading.

During the 1960s, Wilson became involved in the civil rights movement. In 1968, he founded the Black Horizons Theater Company, a community theater in Pittsburgh devoted to addressing the problems of African Americans. In 1978 he moved to Minneapolis and began writing plays for a small theater company.

August Wilson is one of the leading African American playwrights of this age. Wilson's powerful narratives are noted for their humor and dialogue, which blend lively colloquial phrases and poetic monologues.

In 1985, Wilson's first major work, *Ma Rainey's Black Bottom* (1984), shows White promoters exploiting a Black recording artist in the 1920s. This play won the New York Drama Critics award for best play. Wilson's other plays include *Seven Guitars* (1995); *Joe Turner's Come and Gone* (1988); *Two Trains Running* (1992); and *Jitney* (1982). Wilson also won two Pulitzer Prizes; one in 1987, for *Fences* (written in 1985); the story of a Black sanitation worker who is denied the chance to play major league baseball, and the other in 1990, for *The Piano Lesson* (written in 1987); a drama set in 1936, about a brother and sister who disagree over whether to sell or keep the family heirloom, a richly carved piano that is a symbol of the family's heritage of slavery.

Wilson's plays often deal with the conflict between Blacks who accept mainstream American culture and Blacks who want to embrace their African heritage. Along with his two Pulitzer Prizes, he is also the recipient of a Tony Award, five New York Drama Circle Awards, and many other accolades.

He is married and they have one child.

Lorraine Hansberry
(1930–1965)

AUTHOR

Lorraine Hansberry, the first African American playwright to achieve critical and political success on Broadway, was born May 19, 1930, in Chicago, Illinois, to a well-to-do middle-class family. Her family owned a successful real estate firm and one of the first African American-owned banks in Chicago. Because of the family's status in the community, the Hansberry home was frequented by such luminaries as Walter White, Jesse Owens, Langston Hughes, Duke Ellington, and Paul Robeson.

Hansberry attended the University of Wisconsin from 1948 to 1950, studying English and stage design. In 1950, she moved to New York City, where she got a part-time job as associate editor for Paul Robeson's Harlem-based magazine, *Freedom*. She remained until 1953. Perfecting her skills as a writer, she wrote articles dealing with Africa, women's and social issues.

She also reviewed plays, which motivated her to write her own plays. Her first play, *A Raisin in the Sun*, written in 1959, was the first drama by a Black woman to be produced on Broadway. *A Raisin in the Sun* is the story of one man's search for identity within a racially prejudiced American society, At the age of twenty-nine, Hansberry received the New York Drama Critics Circle Award. She was the youngest playwright, the fifth woman, and the first African American to receive the honor. The original Broadway cast, which included Sidney Poitier, Ruby Dee, Diana Sands, and Claudia McNeil, also starred in the 1961 film version of the play. Hansberry received many special awards at the 1961 Cannes Film Festival, including Best Picture.

After the overwhelming success of *A Raisin in the Sun*, Hansberry worked on numerous uncompleted projects, including a novel and a collection of essays. Her last completed stage work, *The Sign in Sidney Brustein's Window*, written in 1964 and set in Greenwich Village, tells the story of a Jewish liberal whose commitment to various social causes almost ruins his marriage. The play remained on Broadway for 101 performances.

Unfortunately, Hansberry's young life was cut short at the age of 34 by cancer. Before her death, Hansberry had begun a play about race relations in Africa. The unfinished work was published as *Les Blancs* in 1970. *To Be Young Gifted and Black*, completed by Robert Nemieroff from her writings, was produced off-Broadway in 1969 and published in book form in 1970 as a part of her biography. Lorraine Hansberry died on January 12, 1965, in New York City.

Alex Haley
(1921–1992)
AUTHOR

Alex Haley was born in Ithaca, New York. His father was a professor and his mother was an elementary school teacher. They would spend summers in Henning, Tennessee, with their relatives. Haley would often hear his grandmother talk about her ancestors, including a slave named Toby.

Haley completed two years at Elizabeth City Teachers College. He was going to follow in his parent's footsteps and pursue a career in education, but instead, he dropped out and joined the Coast Guard. He rose from the low position of kitchen mess boy to chief journalist, a position they created exclusively for Haley. Alex loved to write, and he chronicled the Coast Guard's activities. Haley retired from the Coast Guard after completing a 20-year stint.

In 1959, Haley embarked on a professional writing career. He submitted articles to many magazines and received many rejection letters. At one point he was so poor he was down to 18 cents and a couple of cans of sardines. Later, he framed them as a reminder of his determination.

In 1962, Haley interviewed Malcolm X for a magazine article. They developed mutual admiration for each other, and Malcolm X asked him to collaborate on an autobiography. Haley spent a year interviewing Malcolm X, and the project was completed two weeks before Malcolm X was assassinated. The book has sold more than seven million copies since its release in 1965. In an interview with *Essence*, Haley said, "I'm glad the book exists because many people said they knew or worked with Malcolm and never did."

After Malcolm X, Haley wanted to explore his own roots and research more about his grandmother's reference to Toby. Alex spent nine years researching his family history. He investigated city records, museums, libraries, and Gambia in West Africa. In 1976, *Roots: The Saga of an American Family*, was released. He won a Pulitzer prize and the National Book Award. The book sold more than 10 million copies and been translated into 30 languages. The movie version of the book was viewed by 130 million Americans or half the United States population. Roots inspired families of all races to look into their history.

Suddenly, Haley was in demand as a speaker. In one year he conducted 226 speeches. His demanding career took a toll on his family life and his health. He was married three times, and each wife expressed concern that Haley was married to his work and not them. He died of a heart attack en route to a speaking engagement February 10, 1992.

His estate in Tennessee has been developed by Marian Edelman and the Children's Defense Fund into a retreat to develop young African American leaders.

Before his death, Haley was working on a story about his grandmother, a slave named Queen. CBS-TV developed it into a miniseries, *Alex Haley's Queen.*

Haley is survived by three children.

Alice Walker
(1944–)
AUTHOR

Alice Walker was born the youngest of eight children in Eatonton, Georgia. At the age of eight her brother shot her in the eye with a BB bullet. Because her family was poor and did not own a car, Walker was forced to wait a week before the doctor arrived. He told her she would be permanently blind in one eye.

Walker graduated from high school as valedictorian and senior class queen. She was awarded a scholarship to Spelman College. She left after her sophomore year and enrolled in and graduated from Sarah Lawrence College in Bronxville, New York in 1965. She spent one summer in Africa, which greatly affected her future writing. She taught after graduation at Jackson State University and Tougaloo College.

Walker has been prolific over the past three decades. Her first book was *The Third Life of Grange Copeland (1967)*. Other books include *In Love and Trouble; Revolutionary Petunias and Other Poems; The Life of Thomas Hodge; Langston Hughes, American Poet; Meridian; Good Night Willie Lee; I'll See You in the Morning; I Love Myself When I Am Laughing; You Can't Keep a Good Woman Down; The Temple of My Familiar; Houses Make a Landscape Look More Beautiful; Living by the Word; In Search of Our Mothers' Gardens; Finding the Green Stone; Her Blue Body; Possessing the Secret of Joy; Warrior Marks; The Same River Twice; Anything We Love Can Be Saved; By the Light of My Father's Smile*, and many more.

Walker's best-selling book was *The Color Purple*, which was released in 1983. It won her the Pulitzer Prize, the American Book Award, and many other awards. Warner Brothers paid her handsomely for the movie rights. The movie was a blockbuster and received eleven Academy Award nominations.

She prefers the term "womanist" over "feminist." Walker has been offered many academic awards and honorary degrees, but she has generally refused them, valuing instead the satisfaction she derives from exploring the African American experience.

She has one daughter.

Toni Morrison
(1931–)
AUTHOR AND EDUCATOR

Toni Morrison was born Chloe Anthony Wofford in Lorraine, Ohio, the second of four children. Her father was a major influence on her life. He was a very proud man who sought excellence in his work as a shipyard welder. He worked three jobs to provide for his family. Not surprisingly, she loved to read and was the only child to enter first grade with above-level reading skills. She read French and Russian novelists and Latin in high school and graduated with honors.

Unlike her peers, who stayed home and married, Morrison enrolled at Howard University. She majored in English and minored in the Classics. She changed her named to Toni, a shortened version of her middle name because many people could not pronounce her first name. After graduation in 1953, she pursued her master's degree at Cornell University. Her thesis focused on the works of William Faulkner and Virginia Woolf. After graduation in 1955, she taught at Texas Southern University and later in 1957 at Howard University. Her students included Claude Brown and Stokely Carmichael. She married Harold Morrison in 1957, and they had two sons. Unfortunately, they divorced in 1964.

In 1965, Morrison accepted a position as textbook editor for Random House. In 1968, she was promoted to senior editor in the trade department. During her tenure, which continued through 1983, she secured for Random House writers such as Toni Cade Bambara, Angela Davis, Henry Dumas, Leon Forrest, Gayl Jones, and many others. Morrison continued to teach at the University of New York at Purchase, Yale University, and Bard College.

In 1984, Morrison left the publishing world and accepted the Albert Schweitzer Chair of Humanities at the University of New York at Albany. In 1989 she became the first African American woman to hold a named chair (Robert Goheen) in an Ivy League university.

In 1965, she wrote a college textbook. Her first novel, *The Bluest Eye,* was released in 1970. *Sula* came in 1974, *Song of Solomon* in 1977, and *Tar Baby* in 1981.

Morrison won the 1987 Pulitzer Prize for *Beloved.* This powerful work describes the horrible effects of slavery on the psyche of some mothers and their children. Oprah Winfrey was so moved that she bought the movie rights and spent $50 million to produce the movie version. Morrison became the first African American to win the Nobel Prize in Literature in 1993. In 1998, she released the best-selling book *Paradise.* This excellent book parallels an all Black town to the Biblical *Exodus* and much more. Morrison has won many awards for *Paradise.*

Morrison is on many boards. She is co-chairperson for the Schaumburg Library and the Commission for the Preservation of Black Culture.

Nikki Giovanni
(1943–)
AUTHOR

Nikki Giovanni was born Yolande Cornelia Giovanni, Jr., on June 7, 1943, in Knoxville, Tennessee, the second child of Yolande and Jones Giovanni. In August of that same year, the Giovanni family moved to Cincinnati, Ohio. In 1957, she moved back to Knoxville to live with her maternal grandparents, Emma Louvenia and John Brown Watson, and attended Austin High School.

In 1960, Giovanni entered Fisk University in Nashville, Tennessee. But after her grandfather's death in February 1961, she left Fisk and returned to Cincinnati. There she got a job at Walgreen's and took occasional classes at the University of Cincinnati.

In 1964, Giovanni returned to Fisk University. She reestablished the Student Nonviolent Coordinating Committee (SNCC) chapter at the school. Later, in 1966, she became John O. Killen's assistant in his writer's workshop. In 1967, Giovanni graduated from Fisk University, receiving her bachelor of arts degree.

That same year, she organized the first Cincinnati Black Arts Festival and became the managing editor of *Conversation*. She later attended the Detroit Conference of Unity and Art, and entered the University of Pennsylvania's School of Social Work with a Ford Foundation fellowship.

In 1968, she moved to New York City. While there, she received a scholarship from the National Foundation of the Arts to attend Columbia University's School of Fine Arts and to publish her first book, *Black Feeling, Black Talk*. In 1969, she published her second book, *Black Judgement,* with a grant from the Harlem Council of the Arts. She also taught at Queens College and Rutgers University.

Throughout the 1970s, 1980s, and 1990s, Nikki Giovanni published and edited many books and anthologies of poetry, and has released five spoken word albums. She has traveled extensively throughout the United States, Africa, and Europe. Throughout her life and career, she has received many awards and honorary doctorates.

In 1987, Giovanni was invited to be Commonwealth Visiting Professor of English at Virginia Polytechnic Institute and State University in Blacksburg. In 1989, she accepted the position permanently. Over the past decade, she has written *Genie in the Jar; Shimmy Shimmy Shimmy: Looking at the Harlem Renaissance; The Women and the Men; Racism 101; Love Poems; Grandmother Poems;* and *Grandfather Poems.*

Giovanni has one son.

Susan Taylor
(1946–)
EDITOR AND AUTHOR

Susan Taylor was born in Harlem, New York. She was the daughter of blue-collar parents. Her public career began in the 1960s as an actress in The Negro Ensemble Company. In 1969, she gave birth to her daughter, Shana Nequia, and gave up her acting career. In order to spend more time with her daughter, she became a licensed beautician and created her own cosmetics line (Nequia Cosmetics).

In 1970, *Essence* became the first life-style magazine devoted to Black women. Taylor said, "I was so happy I didn't know whether to read it or hug it." She worked for *Essence* as a freelance beauty writer in 1970. Times were tough for Susan and Shana financially. She earned $500 a month and paid $368 a month in rent.

Taylor grew with *Essence*. She became editor for the beauty and fashion departments. In 1980, she became editor-in-chief and began writing the highly acclaimed column "In the Spirit." The circulation and readership continue to grow. The circulation approaches a million subscribers.

In 1986, Taylor was promoted to vice president of *Essence* communications. This new position allowed her to host and produce the *Essence* television show. She also produces the *Essence Awards* and the Essence Festival and Seminars.

She compiled her "In the Spirit" editorials into a best-selling book with the same title. She also wrote *Lessons in Living* and co-authored with her husband *Confirmation: The Spiritual Wisdom that has Shaped Our Lives*. Taylor earned her bachelor's degree in social science and economics from Fordham University in 1990. She has received numerous awards for her journalism and management skills.

Maya Angelou
(1928–)
AUTHOR

Maya Angelou was born Marguerite Johnson on April 4, 1928, in St. Louis, Missouri. She and her brother Bailey were raised by her paternal grandparents in segregated rural Arkansas. She moved to her mother's home in San Francisco after graduating with honors from Lafayette County Training School in 1940. At age sixteen, she graduated from high school, gave birth to her son Guy, and began a series of jobs, including stints as a cook and waitress. Angelou speaks French, Spanish, Italian, and West African Fanti. She began her career in drama and dance in 1949. In the 1950s, she became a nightclub performer and began successful careers as singer, dancer, actor, playwright, magazine editor, civil rights activist, poet, and novelist. She married a South African freedom fighter, Tosh Angelou. They lived in Cairo, and she was editor of the *Arab Observer*, the only English-language news weekly in the Middle East. In Ghana, she was the feature editor of the *African Review* and taught at the University of Ghana.

At the request of Martin Luther King, Jr., Angelou became the northern coordinator for the Southern Christian Leadership Conference in 1960. She was appointed by President Gerald Ford to the Bicentennial Commission and by President Jimmy Carter to the National Commission on the Observance of International Women's Year.

In the film industry, through her work in scriptwriting and directing, Angelou has been a groundbreaker for Black women. In television, she has make hundreds of appearances. Her best-selling autobiographical account of her youth, *I Know Why the Caged Bird Sings*, won critical acclaim in 1970 and was a two-hour television special on CBS. It was the first of a four-book series about her life that also included *Gather Together in My Name* (1974), *Singin' and Swingin' and Gettin' Merry Like Christmas* (1976), and *The Heart of a Woman* (1981). She has written and produced several prizewinning documentaries, including "Afro-Americans in the Arts," a PBS special for which she received the Golden Eagle Award. She was also nominated for an Emmy Award for her acting in *Roots* and her screenplay *Georgia. Georgia*, was the first screenplay by a Black woman to be filmed.

Angelou has received many awards and honorary degrees. Some of her other works include *Just Give Me a Cool Drink of Water 'fore I Die, the Poetry of Maya Angelou* (1971); *Oh Pray My Wings Are Gonna Fit Me Well* (1975); *And Still I Rise* (1978); *Shaker, Why Don't You Sing?* (1983); *All God's Children Need Traveling Shoes* (1986); *Now Sheba Sings the Song* (1987); *I Shall Not Be Moved* (1990); and *Wouldn't Take Nothing for My Journey Now* (1993). In 1993, she read her poem "On the Pulse of Morning" at the inauguration of President Bill Clinton. Her latter books are *A Collection of Poems; Even the Stars Look Lonesome;* and *The Heart of a Woman*. In 1999, she directed *Down in the Delta*.

Angelou has been a professor at Wake Forest University since 1981.

Zora Neale Hurston
(1891–1960)
AUTHOR

Zora Neale Hurston was born in Eatonville, Florida, the first incorporated Black township in the United States. Her father was elected mayor three times. Her mother was a schoolteacher and raised eight children.

Hurston left Eatonville at fourteen and completed high school in Baltimore. She took some college classes at Howard. She had a burning desire to participate in the Harlem Renaissance, so she migrated to New York in 1925. She graduated from Barnard in 1928 and took graduate classes at Columbia. She was encouraged by her anthropology professor, Frank Boas, to return to Eatonville and collect Black folklore. *Mules and Men* is her folklore collection and represents the first assembled by an African American.

In 1937, Hurston released what critics felt is her best work, *Their Eyes Were Watching God.* It was written in seven weeks in the Caribbean after a love affair ended. The book describes the challenge of a Black woman's search for identity beyond a small rural town.

In 1942, *Dust Tracks* was released and it received many awards, including the Anisfield-Wolf Award for its contribution to better race relations. The book is a combination of autobiography and folklore. She refused to complain about the social plight of Black people. She said she was too busy trying to improve her craft.

Her other books included *Tell My Horse; Moses, Man of the Mountain;* and *Seraph on the Suwanee.* These books received a mild response. Hurston wrote numerous articles for magazines and journals.

In 1950, Hurston wrote an article entitled, "What White Publishers Won't Print." Hurston was very disappointed at the rigid stereotypes White publishers enforced on Black writers. Her income and health declined in the 1950s and she died in poverty. Alice Walker, who refers to Hurston as her literary foremother, traveled to her Florida gravesite and placed a stone marker on her grave in 1973.

Rita Dove
(1952–)
POET

Rita Dove was born in Akron, Ohio, with three other siblings. Her father was the first African American chemist to work in the tire and rubber industry. Dove was a brilliant student. She visited the White House in 1970 as one of the top 100 high school students in the country. She attended Miami University in Oxford, Ohio, and graduated with honors in 1973. She majored in English and found her love and passion in poetry. She earned her master's degree from the University of Iowa in 1977. From 1981 to 1989 she taught at Arizona State University. Currently, she is a professor at the University of Virginia.

Dove loves to write and is very disciplined. She writes for six hours every day of the week. Her first book of poetry was *The Yellow House* (1980). *Museum* was released in 1983 and received rave reviews. Her most respected work, *Thomas and Beulah* (1986), describes African American life in the early 1900s and was inspired by her grandparents. She won a Pulitzer Prize and the Academy of American Poets Award for this fantastic publication. Her fourth book of poems, *Grace Notes* (1990), reflects her childhood and nursing her daughter.

Her debut novel, *Through the Ivory Gate* (1992), is about a gifted woman who returns to her community to teach and inspire children. In 1993, Dove became the youngest poet to serve as Poet Laureate for the United States. Dove is the third African American to hold this prestigious position. She was preceded by Robert Hayden and Gwendolyn Brooks. She held the position from 1993 to 1995 and motivated many people to pursue their dreams in literature.

Dove's works include *Fifth Sunday; Museum on the Bus with Rosa Parks; Selected Poems; The Darker Face of the Earth,* and *Mother Love Poems.* Rita is married and has one child.

Amiri Baraka

(1934–)

AUTHOR

Originally named Everet LeRoi Jones, Baraka changed his name to Imamu Ameer Baraka in 1968. In the 1970s, he altered this name to Amiri Baraka. Born in Newark, New Jersey, he was one of the country's leading black intellectuals of the 1960s. He earned a scholarship to Rutgers University in 1951, but transferred a year later to Howard University, where he earned his bachelor's degree in 1954. After serving three years in the Air Force, he settled in New York City's Greenwich Village, where he befriended several prominent Beat Generation poets, including Allen Ginsberg.

In 1958, Baraka founded *Yugen,* a radical poetry journal. In 1964, his first major play, *The Dutchman*, opened in New York and won an Obie Award. Both *The Dutchman* and his second major play, *The Slave*, dealt with the corrosive effects of racism. Also, in 1964, he founded the Black Arts Repertory Theater.

Throughout the late 1960s, Baraka's poems, novels, plays, and essays were a major force in pushing African American literature away from themes of integration toward a focus on the black experience. In the 1970s, he turned more toward politics, founding the Congress of African People and organizing the Black National Political Convention in 1972. In 1974, he abandoned the black nationalist movement in favor of Marxism and Lennism. In 1983, after having held teaching posts at Yale and Columbia universities, he became chair of the African Studies program at the State University of New York at Stony Brook.

Amiri Baraka has been prolific over the past three decades. His writings include *Black Magic; Black Music; Wise Why's Y's: The Griot Tale; A Nation Within A Nation; Transbluesency; Home: Social Essays; Four Black Revolutionary Plays; Eulogies; Conversations with Baraka; Autobiography of Leroi Jones; Funk Lore: New Poems;* among others.

He is married and has seven children.

James Baldwin
(1924–1987)
AUTHOR

Born in Harlem New York, Baldwin was the oldest of nine children in a very poor family. Baldwin's stepfather was a preacher who demanded that his children follow a strict set of rules. An excellent student, Baldwin was more interested in academics than in running the streets. Baldwin loved reading.

When Baldwin was fourteen, he went through a religious experience where he felt he was being called to preach the word of God. He became a junior minister in his father's Pentecostal church. Although this period would later serve as a great influence on his writings, Baldwin began to question the teaching of Christianity.

Baldwin wrote six novels, four plays, and seven collections of essays. His first novel, *Go Tell it on the Mountain,* is generally regarded as his best. He followed this with *Notes of a Native Son, Giovanni's Room* and *Another Country.* In 1968, Baldwin's popular novel *Tell Me How Long the Train's Been Gone* was released. *A Rap on Race* articulated his views on racism in 1971. In 1974, his best-seller was *If Beale Street Could Talk,* the tale of a pregnant unmarried 19-year-old. His plays include *The Amen Corner* and *Blues for Mister Charley.*

Baldwin went on to become what he would call "a disturber of the peace" due to his refusal to allow the American public to remain apathetic about some of the social issues which were threatening to tear the country apart. However, the brutal murders of three of his friends working on behalf of civil rights—Medgar Evers, Martin Luther King, and Malcolm X put a dark cloud over his hopes for racial unity in America. Baldwin made France his permanent home in the early 1970s.

In 1987, he received the French Legion Honor award. Baldwin died of stomach cancer in France the same year. At his funeral, poet Amiri Baraka reflected on his life by saying that Baldwin had "traveled the earth like its history and biographer. He reported, criticized, made beautiful, analyzed, cajoled, lyricized, attacked, sang, made us think, made us better, made us consciously human."

Charlayne Hunter Gault
(1942–)

JOURNALIST

Charlayne Hunter Gault was born in Due West, South Carolina, and has two siblings. Her childhood was split between South Carolina, Atlanta, and Alaska. Her grandmother, who possessed a third grade education, sparked her interest by reading three newspapers daily.

Gault desired to be a journalist, but the only school in Georgia offering a degree in her field was very segregated—the University of Georgia. She attended Wayne State in Detroit for three semesters before the courts abolished segregation. She and Hamilton Holmes were the first African American students admitted to the University of Georgia. There were riots and protests throughout the year, and they were always in danger. Gault would return to the school twenty-seven years later to give the commencement address. This was another first for an African American.

After graduation in 1963, Gault worked at the *New Yorker* and *Trans-Action* magazines and later for WRC-TV in Washington. In 1968, she joined the *New York Times* and specialized in stories about Harlem. She fought and convinced her editors to use Black rather than Negro. She remained there for a decade and won many awards, including the George Foster Peabody Award.

In 1978, she became a correspondent for the *MacNeil/Lehrer News Hour.* Five years later, she became a national correspondent and part-time anchor. She interviewed major figures, including Desmond Tutu, Bill Cosby, George Bush, Margaret Thatcher, and Norman Schwarzkopf. Gault won an Emmy for her Grenada coverage in 1983, and in 1986, was named Journalist of the Year by the National Association of Black Journalists. She also won the George Foster Peabody award that same year.

In 1992 she released her highly acclaimed autobiography, *In My Place,* which enhanced racial understanding and relations. Gault remained with MacNeil/Lehrer for two decades. In 1998, her husband's banking business transferred him to South Africa. Gault followed and became a correspondent with National Public Radio. Her Peabody Award winning series was on life in South Africa and Apartheid.

Gault and her husband have two children.

Oprah Winfrey
(1954–)
TALK-SHOW HOST

Oprah Winfrey was born on January 29, 1954, in Kosciusko, Mississippi, to unwed teenage parents, who separated after her birth. Winfrey spent her troubled childhood living in extreme poverty on her Bible-thumping grandmother's farm. As a preteen, she moved to Milwaukee to live with her mother, Vernita Lee, under whose roof she was sexually molested several times by male relatives. Winfrey spent her early teens in and out of trouble. At age fourteen, she gave birth to a premature baby, who died shortly thereafter. Facing a threat of being sent to a home for wayward youth, she went to live with her father in Nashville, Tennessee. Vernon Winfrey, a barber and businessman, provided the discipline that was sorely lacking in his daughter's life. He instituted a strict curfew and stressed the value of education. Under his iron fist, Winfrey turned her life around in record time.

At age nineteen, Winfrey landed her first broadcasting job—as a reporter at radio station WVOL in Nashville—and enrolled at Tennessee State University, on a full scholarship, to study speech and the performing arts. In 1972, during her sophomore year, she switched mediums and became the first African American anchor at Nashville's WTVF-TV. After graduation, she was hired as a television newscaster, and later as a Baltimore's television talk show host on Baltimore, Maryland's *People Are Talking*. In 1984, after being at WJZ for eight years, she accepted a job as the host for *A.M. Chicago*. In 1985, the show was renamed *The Oprah Winfrey Show*. Dealing openly with controversial subjects, the show achieved syndication in 1986.

Winfrey, who had always wanted to be an actress but had no professional experience, then landed a plum movie assignment playing the world-weary Sofia in Steven Spielberg's 1985 cinematic adaptation of Alice Walker's Pulitzer Prize winning novel, *The Color Purple*. She won an Academy Award for Best Supporting Actress. In 1998, she starred in *Beloved*, a film acquired by her company. The movie was produced with a $50 million budget.

Shortly thereafter, Winfrey established Harpo Studios, and eventually purchased her program outright from Capital Cities/ABC. As a result, Winfrey became the third woman in history to own a major studio, and is on her way to becoming America's first Black billionaire. She earns more than $100 million per year.

In 1994, President Clinton signed the "Oprah Bill," a law designed to protect children from abuse. In 1998, she successfully defeated the Cattlemen Association who sued her for making an unflattering comment about beef. Her book of the month club has become the bible of the book publishing industry.

Winfrey shares her remarkable good fortune—with hundreds of charities, including her alma mater, Tennessee State University, Morehouse College, and her Family for Better Lives Foundation.

Oprah has also tackled her weight problems with a change in lifestyle consisting of low-fat foods and exercising. She has inspired thousands of others with two books co-authored with her chef, Rosie Daley and her exercise guru Bob Greene.

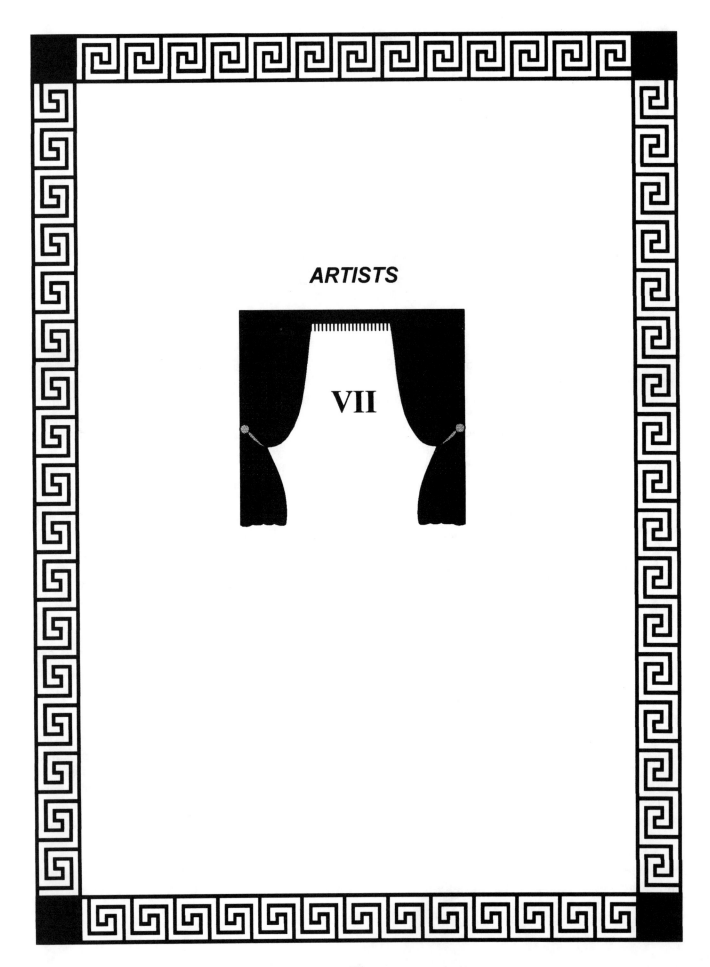

ARTISTS

VII

James Van Der Zee

(1886–1983)

PHOTOGRAPHER

Born in Lenox, Massachusetts, James Van Der Zee was only twelve years old when he won his first camera, a simple box camera, by selling 20 packets of perfume. He experimented many times with his new gift, and in a short time he became proficient at using more complex cameras. Photography intrigued him, but it wasn't until later on in his life that he considered pursuing it professionally.

In 1906, he arrived in Harlem, where he met and married his first wife, Kate Brown. Shortly after the wedding, the two moved to Phoebus, Virginia, where Van Der Zee worked as a busboy. In his spare time, he would photograph the people of Phoebus and nearby Hampton. By the end of 1906, Van Der Zee returned to New York to pursue his true vocation: music.

Dedicated to his music, Van Der Zee rarely photographed the New York scene. But on frequent trips back to his hometown, he photographed his family and friends, which rekindled his love for the art. By 1915, his career as a musician was languishing. So he decided to get a job as a darkroom technician in the Gertz Department Store in Newark, New Jersey, for about five dollars a week, in order to make ends meet. Frequently required to fill in as a photographer, Van Der Zee created poses for his clients, making him exceedingly popular. The opportunity allowed him to gain invaluable technical experience. As a result, he was able to open his own studio on 135th Street in Harlem, called Guaranty Photo. His unique window displays attracted many local residents as well as curious visitors to Harlem.

Thereafter, Van Der Zee earned his living by making portraits. He enjoyed considerable success, both artistically and financially. By 1932, he opened up a larger studio, GGG Studio, with his second wife and partner Gaynella.

Van Der Zee's legacy as a photographer lies not so much in the artistic value of his photographs as in his willingness to photograph Harlemites in the studio or on location. There is simply no aspect of Harlem that was overlooked by Van Der Zee. During the 1920s and 1930s, Harlem became a haven for artists, musicians, politicians, entrepreneurs, and newly migrated Blacks from the South and the West Indies. Van Der Zee photographed all the important people and events. In his collection are photographs of Henry Johnson and Needham Roberts, the first Black Americans in the Army of France to receive the Croix de Guerre; singers Mamie Smith, Hazel Scott, and Florence Mills; poet Countee Cullen; heavyweight boxing champions Jack Johnson, Joe Louis, and Harry Wills; religious leaders Adam Clayton Powell, Sr. and Jr., Father Divine, and Daddy Grace; and the heiress and patron A'Lelia Walker, daughter of Black millionaire Madame C. J. Walker. He was also the official photographer for Marcus Garvey and the Universal Negro Improvement Association (UNIA).

In 1969, the Metropolitan Museum of Art presented *Harlem on My Mind*, an exhibition on Harlem in the 20th century. Van Der Zee's collection was the largest photographic contribution to the exhibition; he was introduced to the public as one of the most important photographers of New York's and America's history.

Meta Vaux Warrick Fuller
(1877-1968)
ARTIST

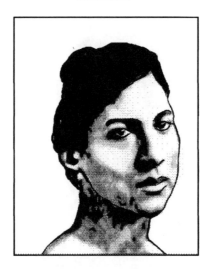

Reared in a Black middle-class Philadelphia home, Meta Vaux Warrick Fuller attended the Pennsylvania Museum and School for Industrial Arts (now known as the Philadelphia College of Art) from 1894 to 1899. Although in 1903 she continued her education at the Pennsylvania Academy of the Fine Arts, by 1902 she had already become an established artist in Paris.

While in Paris, Fuller studied with sculptor Auguste Rodin, whose strong influence is reflected in her art. She emphasized romance. For inspiration, Fuller looked to Black American songs and African folktales that were filled with themes of passion and joy. She introduced America to the power of Black American and African subjects even before the Harlem Renaissance began. Until Fuller, the aesthetics of the Black visual artist was inextricably tied to the taste of White America, and even more so to the definitions of form and subject matter derived from European art. Outside of Edmonia Lewis' *Forever Free* (1867) and Henry O. Tanner's *Banjo Lesson* (1893) and *The Thankful Poor* (1894), very little in the nineteenth century art had been created with Black or African themes.

In 1914, Fuller created a piece which symbolized the development of the "New Negro." This sculpture anticipated the spirit and style of the Harlem Renaissance. The piece was entitled *Ethiopia Awakening*. It awakened Black America to the consciousness of nationhood and anticolonialism.

In Paris, during the early 1900s, Fuller met with W. E. B. DuBois and became devoted to understanding the full range of race relations in Europe and America. Her insights were reflected in her artistic creations. In addition to her preoccupation with Black themes, she dealt extensively with themes of death and sorrow. Critics often referred to her work as macabre and highly emotional. Fuller's art demonstrates her astute observance of history and her insightful understanding that Black subject matter could be meaningful in the work of Black artists.

She is survived by three sons.

Palmer Hayden
(1890–1973)
ARTIST

Born Peyton Hedgeman in Wide Water, Virginia, Palmer Hayden is often referred to as a self-trained artist, although records show that he studied at Cooper Union in New York City and pursued independent study at Boothbay Art Colony in Maine. He also studied and painted independently in France, where he lived from 1927 to 1932. Hayden's reputation derives from his realistic depictions of folklore and Black historical events. Like Aaron Douglas, Hayden was one of the first Black artists to use African subjects and designs in his paintings. Although he was praised by Alain Locke for his modernist approach to painting, Hayden was not a modernist. Instead, he broke away from tradition by depicting African art in his paintings.

Hayden worked for many years and remained loyal of the Harmon Foundation, where he exhibited many times from the beginning of 1926. Most of Hayden's works depict Black people in the comfortable and humble surroundings in which they lived. Other images exhibit African American's devotion to public service. One example is an autobiographical piece entitled *The Janitor Who Paints* (1939).

The styles and manners of the people he painted are important elements in Hayden's art. His paintings of the 1930s and 1940s chronicle the style of dress found in the Black rural South and northern urban communities. They culturally depict print designs, women's hairstyles, and the flamboyant fashions associated with northern Black men. One example is his piece entitled *Just back From Washington* (1938), which represents the "city dude," a perennial presence at the nightspots of Harlem during the 1930s and 1940s.

Often his images were exaggerated, with stylized eyes, noses, lips, and ears, and the heads were often bald and round in form. He explained that the basis for his inspiration came from Black folk tradition and its heroes, such as John Henry. Hayden insisted that he was painting an era in history, and his works symbolized the comedy, tragedy, and pleasures of a Black lifestyle during that era.

Barbara Chase-Ribond
(1939–)
ARTIST

Barbara Chase-Ribond was born in Philadelphia. She began working as a child in sculpture and ceramics at the Fletcher Art Memorial School and won first prize in sculpture at the age of eight. She also studied at the Philadelphia Museum School of Art. At age fifteen, she won a *Seventeen* magazine award for one of her prints, which was purchased and displayed at the Museum of Modern Art in New York. She earned a B.F.A. from Temple University in 1957 and a M.F.A. from Yale in 1960.

Ribond would not be confined to the United States. She studied at the American Academy in Rome for one year. In Egypt she not only discovered her roots but that Greece and Rome were not the origins of civilization. She received a much deeper appreciation of African civilization as she viewed the pyramids and temples. She lives in Paris.

Her art work was showcased in the Pan-African festival in Algeria in 1966 and in Nigeria in 1969. She was greatly influenced by Malcolm X, and she developed an exhibition in his honor featured at the Massachusetts Institute of Technology in 1969–1970. Her art has been featured at hundreds of galleries.

Ribond's sculptures consist of bronze, wool, steel, synthetics, silk, leather, hemp, and feathers. Her sculptures are powerful studies in contrasts—unyielding metals supported by braided, knotted, and wrapped fibers.

Ribond has written two powerful novels—*Sally Hemmings* (1979) and *Echo of Lions* in 1980. The first about Thomas Jefferson's Black mistress which won several awards. The latter about Joseph Cinque and the *Amistad*.

She is married with two children.

Aaron Douglas

(1899–1979)

ARTIST

Aaron Douglas arrived in Harlem in 1924 with a bachelor's degree in art education from the University of Nebraska in Lincoln. After a year of teaching high school in Kansas City, Douglas was convinced that he had a higher calling in art elsewhere. Douglas made one of America's most worthy contributions to art, by helping the Harlem Renaissance get under way.

After arriving in New York City, he met German artist Winold Reiss, who suggested that he look into African art for design elements "that would express racial commitment in his art." His exploration and use of Black subject matter in his work brought him to the attention of such Black leaders, scholars, and activists as W.E.B. DuBois and Alain Locke. DuBois invited him to contribute to *The Crisis* magazine. Soon he was selling his illustrations to *Opportunity, Vanity Fair,* and *Theater Arts Monthly* as well. Alain Locke even used some of his work in his famous anthology of Black writers, *The New Negro* (1925). Douglas soon became labeled as a "pioneering Africanist" and "the father of Black American art," the first such praise and stamp of approval given to a visual artist.

Douglas' reputation quickly spread across the country, and he was quickly sought after by many patrons of the arts to paint murals and historical narratives relating to Black history and racial pride.

One of his most celebrated series of paintings can be found in James Weldon Johnson's book of poems entitled *God's Trombones: Seven Negro Sermons in Verse.* In it he creates his own precisionist style of drawing, derived from the language of Synthetic Cubism, the lyrical style of Winold Reiss, and the forms of African sculpture. As a result of his success, he was frequently invited by other notable authors to illustrate their works as well. The most notable invitation came from Paul Morand, who requested illustrations for his book *Black Magic.*

To capture the essence of Black expression, Douglas would carefully observe the crowds of Blacks swaying back and forth at the Savoy Ballroom and the Dark Tower, clubs where Black socialites gathered to see and to be seen. The prowling artist, amid the sounds of music and excitement around him, began to find the images, if not the subject matter, he needed.

Critics looked upon Douglas' work as "a breath of fresh air" in what had been a rather "stagnant climate." Douglas used geometric formulas in his work. Circles, triangles, rectangles, and squares became the dominant design motifs for many of his works.

Douglas' attempts to combine modernist aesthetics with African ancestral imagery gave him the chance to stylize his art in a way that had never been achieved by Black American artists before him. When Douglas became aware that Black people were beginning to understand their own history and destiny, he began to use Black heritage and racial themes as his subject matter.

Elizabeth Catlett
(1915–)
ARTIST

Elizabeth Catlett was born and raised in Washington, D.C. Her father, a Tuskegee math professor, died before her birth. Her mother recognized her drawing and carving talent at an early age. Catlett's desire was to attend the Carnegie Institute, but segregation denied her. Instead, she entered Howard University, which offered the only art department in a Black college in 1933. She graduated magna cum laude in 1936. She continued her education at the University of Iowa. While she was not allowed to live in the dormitories, she was the first student to earn an M.F.A. in sculpture in 1940.

Catlett taught at PrairieView and Dillard University. Her work was showcased at the Institute of Contemporary Art in Boston, Atlanta University, the Baltimore Museum of Art, the Renaissance Society of the University of Chicago, the Newark Museum, and the Albany Institute of Art, among others. The Julius Rosenwald Foundation awarded Catlett a fellowship to do a series of works honoring Black women.

In 1947, Catlett married Francisco Mova from Mexico. Catlett was suspected of being a Communist. Artists who did not agree with the government were branded by Senator Joseph McCarthy. She was arrested in 1959. Three years later she and her husband fled the United States for Mexico. Catlett said, "I'm a political person and no one can take that from me."

In 1959 she became the first female professor of sculpture at the National School of Fine Arts in San Carlos. She became the chair of the department and remained chair until her retirement in 1973.

Catlett remarked, "I am inspired by Black and Mexican people, my two peoples. Neither the masses of Black nor Mexican people have the time or the money to develop formal aesthetic appreciation. I try to reproduce prints. I believe art should be available to all people."

She and her husband have three children.

William H. Johnson
(1901–1970)
ARTIST

William Johnson was born in rural South Carolina to a poor family. In 1918, William H. Johnson left his home in Florence, South Carolina for New York, just as the Harlem Renaissance was getting underway. He studied at the National Academy of Design under George Luks and Charles Hawthorne. He readied himself for a career in art that would later take him to such places as North Africa and Europe. Hawthorne encouraged Johnson to go to Paris in 1926, and there he settled, painted, and studied the works of modern European masters.

Johnson got his first introduction to art in the cartoons he saw in the local newspaper in Florence, South Carolina. Little did he know that his art interests would take him to such places as Tunisia and Norway. But the skills that he had acquired at the National Academy of Design impressed sympathetic European artists, who encouraged him to remain abroad and devote his life to art.

By 1929 he had developed a style of painting that borrowed heavily from Realism and Impressionism. But it began to change when he came in contact with the works of Paul Cézanne, Georges Rouault, and Chaim Soutine. He also admired the rugged and direct style of painting associated with Vincent Van Gogh's work. His eyes and mind were open to change as he embraced one style of painting after another in search of a permanent way to express himself through his art. By 1930, academic realism no longer played an important part in his work.

Johnson's strong interest in people inspired him to experiment with his painting. He wanted to get rid of the attributes of the trained academic and revert to a style of painting which he later referred to as primitive. The primitive style that Johnson developed in Europe was not the same as the primitive style that he reverted to upon his return to America in 1938.

Harlem became the central theme that emanated from his new style of painting. His new style was described as naïve, primitive, and folk-oriented. By the late 1930s, Johnson's style had permanently moved in that direction, and he had reduced his palette to only four or five colors.

Johnson became increasingly interested in Black subjects that emphasized Christian themes. He changed the course of artistic interpretations of Black American themes in Christianity. His compositions entitled *Nativity* (1939), *Descent from the Cross* (1939), and *Mount Calvary* (1939) presented an all-Black cast as the family of Christ. It soon became clear to the observer that Johnson was integrating religious and social messages in his paintings. From 1938 to 1945, Johnson painted murals that chronicled Black life in Harlem. Unfortunately, in 1946 he became paralyzed and suffered 24 years in a hospital before his death.

Margaret Burroughs
(1917–)

ARTIST

Margaret Burroughs was born in Saint Rose Parish, Louisiana. In 1920, she moved with her family to Chicago. By the time she graduated from high school in 1933, she was participating in local art fairs.

By 1937, Burroughs received certificates for teaching elementary and upper grades, but decided to pursue a career in art instead. In 1940, she became a charter member of Chicago's South Side Community Arts Center, which was created as a part of the Works Progress Administration and dedicated by First Lady Eleanor Roosevelt. The Center was an important location for African Americans to take classes and display their art. Burroughs remained there for twenty years as an officer and trustee.

It wasn't until 1946, when she received her bachelor's degree in art education from the Art Institute of Chicago, that she combined her vocation with her avocation by teaching art at DuSable High School in Chicago. She held the position for twenty-two years.

Burroughs exhibited her works throughout the country, including the annual national showcase of Black art at Atlanta University. Twice (in 1947 and in 1955) she won awards at the showcase for her print and watercolor works. In 1949, she married Charles Burroughs, a writer who lived for seventeen years in the Soviet Union. Starting in the 1950s, Burroughs became internationally successful for her oils and acrylics in Europe and Mexico.

In the late 1960s, after producing a series of works that portrayed great African Americans, including Harriet Tubman, Crispus Attucks, and Frederick Douglass, she wrote a poem to her grandson, Eric Toller, explaining her responsibility for producing the series. Another poem, *What Shall I Tell My Children Who Are Black?* became nationally famous. It refers to a collection of African American folk expressions she had published in 1955.

In 1961, Burroughs opened the Ebony Museum of Negro History in her home, later renaming it the DuSable Museum of African American History. The museum was named in honor of Jean Baptiste Pointe DuSable, the settler and fur trader who founded the city of Chicago. Overwhelming response caused the city to donate an old park building as the new home of the museum. Located in the neighborhood of Hyde Park, it has been the permanent residence of the museum since 1968. The museum houses more than 50,000 artifacts, including Joe Louis' boxing gloves and W.E.B. DuBois' graduation robe.

Burroughs retired as a humanities professor at Chicago's Kennedy-King College in 1979. She became director emeritus of the museum in 1985. The late Mayor Harold Washington appointed her to the Chicago Park District Board in 1986. Burroughs continues to provide tours to Africa.

She has two children.

ATHLETICS

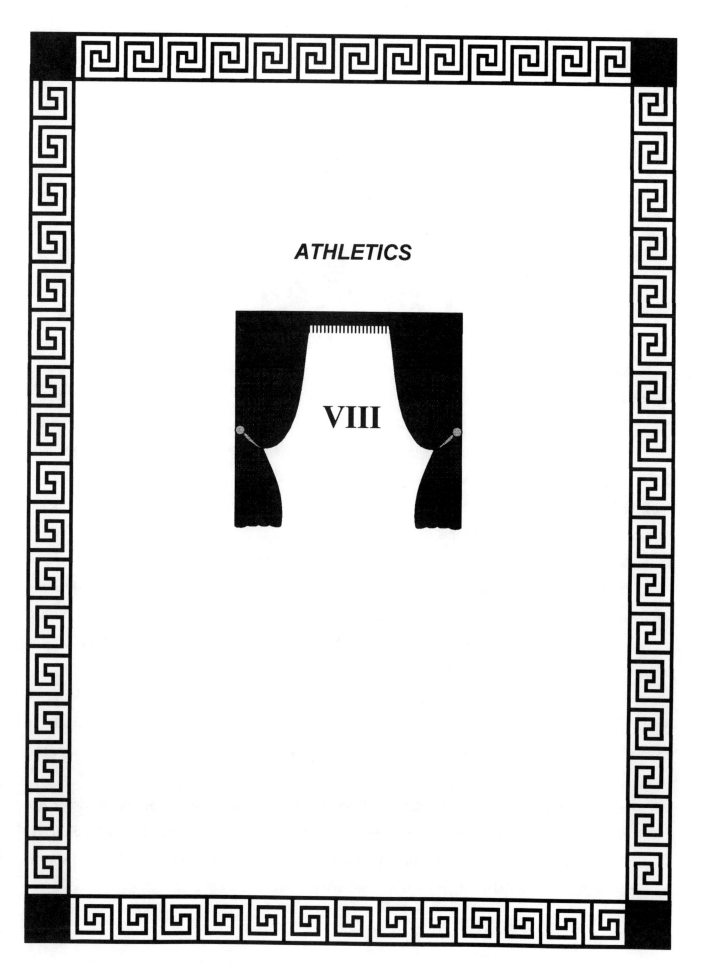

VIII

Sammy Sosa
(1968–)

BASEBALL

Sammy Sosa was born in San Pedro de Macoris, Dominican Republic. He was born in such poverty that he used tree branches for bats and milk cartons for gloves. He sold orange juice and shined shoes for income. His hero was Roberto Clemente, the famous ballplayer for the Pittsburgh Pirates.

At age sixteen, in 1985, he was signed by the Texas Rangers and received a $3,500.00 bonus, which he gave to his mother. He had mediocre seasons with the Rangers, Chicago White Sox, and Chicago Cubs. His career began to blossom in 1993. He became the first Cub to hit more than thirty home runs and steal thirty bases. He has repeated this feat several times.

National attention covered this Dominican Republic star in 1998, when his home runs began to match Roger Maris' record of 61 in a season. The race was even more exciting because Mark McGwire was leading the chase. The season ended with McGwire hitting 70 and Sosa hitting 66. They demolished Maris' record and completely raised the standards. Sammy was gracious and humble throughout the media ordeal, despite many racial discriminations.

Sammy let his on-the-field performance speak for him. He was rewarded the Most Valuable Player Award over McGwire because he had a better average, more runs-batted-in, and the Cubs made the playoff. The voting was not close, and the Chicago Cubs made the playoffs for the first time in two decades.

Sosa remains committed to his homeland. Every time he hits a home run, he offers two kisses, one for his mother and the other for family and friends. He constantly contributes money, and coordinates relief efforts to his homeland. He wears number twenty-one in honor of his hero, the late Roberto Clemente, the famous Pittsburgh outfielder. Sammy is married and they have four children.

Leroy "Satchel" Paige
(1906–1982)
BASEBALL

Satchel Paige is considered the greatest pitcher of all time. His name is synonymous with the Negro Baseball League. The gifted right-handed pitcher from Mobile, Alabama, was a brilliant athlete and entertainer.

His career which spanned four decades, began in 1926 with the Chattanooga Black Lookouts. Over his career he played for the Black Lookouts, Birmingham Black Barons, Nashville Elite Giants, Pittsburgh Crawfords, and Kansas City Monarchs. He only had two pitches, a fastball and a change-up, but the former was so fast it made the change-up almost unhittable. He threw both with pinpoint accuracy. He led the Negro Baseball League in strikeouts almost every year. During one period, he pitched sixty-four scoreless innings and won twenty-one straight victories.

Blacks were not allowed to play in the Major Leagues. Satchel always knew he was just as good as if not better than, Dizzy Dean and Bob Feller, two of the best White pitchers in the Major League. He knew he could strike out Babe Ruth and Lou Gehrig. His primary goal was reaching the Major Leagues.

Throughout his career he would be given the opportunity during exhibition games to compete against his White peers. He faced Dizzy Dean in six exhibition games and the Negro Stars defeated them four times. His team had the same success with Bob Feller. Joe DiMaggio called him the best and fastest pitcher he ever faced.

Finally in 1948, Bill Veeck, the owner of the Cleveland Indians, knew that in order to win the pennant the Indians would need the world's greatest pitcher. Satchel became the oldest rookie to ever play in the major leagues. He was forty-two years old—and still awesome. He won six games and lost only one during the final two months of the season. He also played for the St. Louis Cardinals and Kansas City Athletics.

Paige's final appearance in a major league uniform came twenty-one years later, when he became a coach for the Atlanta Braves in 1969. Always the showman, he brought much attention to the game and attendance increased. In 1971 Satchel Paige was inducted into the Baseball Hall of Fame. He rarely answered questions about his age. His favorite statement was, "Age is a question of mind over matter. If you don't mind, it doesn't matter."

Hank Aaron
(1934–)
BASEBALL

American professional baseball player, Henry Lewis (Hank) Aaron, was born in Mobile, Alabama. During twenty-three seasons in the Major Leagues, from 1954 to 1976, Aaron surpassed many records of some of the greatest hitters of the game, including Babe Ruth, Ty Cobb, and Sam Musial.

Aaron, a right-hander, 6 feet tall and weighing 180 pounds, began his professional career in 1952, playing a few months as a shortstop for the Indianapolis Clowns, in the Negro American League. His contract was bought by the Boston Braves of the National League, who signed him to Minor League teams. After stints in Eau Claire, Wisconsin and Jacksonville, Florida, he joined the Braves in Milwaukee, in 1954.

In 1956 he won the league batting championship with an average of .328. In 1957, he led his team to victory in the World Series and was named the league's Most Valuable Player. Although Aaron played right field for most of his career, he also played left field, center field, and first base. He was a designated hitter his final two seasons.

Before the Braves moved to Atlanta in 1965, Aaron had hit 398 home runs. Aaron led the National League in home runs during the 1957, 1963, 1966, and 1967 seasons. In Atlanta, on April 8, 1974, he hit his 715th home run, breaking Babe Ruth's record (which had stood since 1935). Throughout this record setting year, he received numerous death threats from White supremacists. When Aaron broke the record, he said, "I'm glad it's over."

After the 1974 season, Aaron was traded to the Milwaukee Brewers in the American League. In 1975, he received the Springarn Medal from the NAACP. After the 1976 season, Aaron retired as a player and rejoined the Atlanta Braves as Vice President in charge of Player Development and Scouting. On January 13, 1982, he was elected to the Baseball Hall of Fame with batting records of 755 home runs, 1,477 extra base hits, and 2,297 runs-batted-in. His other career statistics include 2,174 runs scored (second to Ty Cobb); and 12,364 times at bat (second to Pete Rose). His hits (3,771) were exceeded only by Ty Cobb and Pete Rose. Aaron's lifetime batting average was .305.

Aaron is married and has five children.

Venus Williams
(1980–)
TENNIS

Venus Williams, the 5'11" tennis star from Lynwood, California, started playing when she was 4½ years old with her sister Serena under the tutelage of her father, Richard Williams.

Williams comes from a family with a trailblazer spirit. Although tennis is still a sport mostly played by rich White people, Richard Williams didn't let his blue-collar status and lack of experience stop him from training his girls to be the best. Youth who become pros follow the procedures of participation in the amateur youth tournaments. The Williams family ignored these events and emphasized academics and few tournaments. The media would like to suggest that Venus is simply a phenomenon, but she has an almost equally talented sister, Serena, who is also coached by her father.

Venus turned pro when she was almost sixteen. She has excellent range on the court, a fierce backhand, and a record-setting serve of 127 m.p.h. She has risen from a rank of 211 to fifth worldwide. She has amassed more than $2 million in earnings. She has won singles, women's doubles with her sister, and mixed doubles.

The high point in her young career so far was her performance in the 1997 U.S. Open. Although she lost to Martina Hingis, she reached the finals in the tournament. No player had ever gone from being unseeded to the championship. On March 28, 1999, she and her sister played in the Lipton Championship. This had always been their goal. This was the first time in the twentieth century that siblings had played in a championship final.

With her braids with beads, Williams fascinates audiences who enjoy not only her dynamic performances, but her cultural style.

101

Arthur Ashe
(1943–1993)
TENNIS

Arthur Ashe was born in Richmond, Virginia, and began playing tennis when he was six years old. He learned to play very well and won a scholarship to UCLA in 1962. He was selected to play on the U.S. Davis Cup team and was elected captain. He was the first African American to achieve this honor. Upon graduating from UCLA in 1966, he embarked on his professional tennis career.

In 1968, Ashe won the U.S. Open and Wimbledon in 1975. He was ranked number one in the world. Over his career, he won three Grand Slams and more than 800 matches. He was the first African American male to achieve this level of success. Ashe and Althea Gibson were trailblazers. They opened doors and inspired many African American youth to pursue tennis.

Ashe would not be confined to athletics. He was very concerned about apartheid in South Africa. He was a member of TransAfrica and very close to its director, Randall Robinson. He intentionally registered in a tournament knowing that he would be denied. His objective was to bring worldwide attention to this atrocity, and he succeeded.

In 1979, he had open heart surgery. He retired from tennis in 1980. He required further surgery in 1983. It was during one of these procedures that he was given contaminated blood. As his health continued to deteriorate, he was forced by the media to announce he had AIDS. Although this was very traumatic for his wife and daughter, it once again allowed Arthur to bring media attention to a terrible problem. During this era, people thought only homosexuals and drug users got AIDS.

Before his death, Ashe completed a three-volume set, *A Hard Road to Glory,* which chronicled the history of the African American athlete in America. Ashe advocated that athletes receive a good education. He was inducted into the Tennis Hall of Fame in 1994. A monument was built in Richmond in his honor in 1995. A stadium which today hosts the prestigious U.S. Open, was built in New York and named in his honor in 1997.

Ashe is survived by a wife and one daughter.

Althea Gibson
(1927–)
TENNIS

Althea Gibson was born August 25, 1927, in Silver, South Carolina. She later relocated to Harlem with her sharecropper parents. While in New York, she was frequently absent from school—prone to playing hooky and spending her days at the movies.

She was eventually placed in a foster home and became an embittered, restless child who couldn't hold a job. Despite being a malcontent, Gibson showed remarkable skill in street basketball, stickball, and table tennis. One day, a New York City recreation department worker noticed her talents and introduced her to his friend Fred Johnson, a tennis pro at Harlem's elite Cosmopolitan Club.

In 1942, shortly after she won her first tournament at the New York Open Championship, Cosmopolitan Club members put their resources together and sent Gibson to more tournaments. She caught the eye of two doctors, who were leaders in the American Tennis Association (ATA), and they became her sponsors. Beginning in 1947, she won the first of ten ATA National Championships.

Gibson's success in tennis made her a better student. In 1949, she graduated from high school and ranked tenth in her class. She later attended Florida A&M College.

She received invitations to play around the world. In 1950, she became the first African American woman asked to play in the U.S. National Championship Tournament at Forest Hills, now known as the U.S. Open. Although she was eliminated in the second round, she traveled to Europe, Mexico, and Southeast Asia, winning sixteen out of eighteen tournaments, thus securing her bid to Wimbledon.

Gibson was defeated at Wimbledon that year and at Forest Hills for the second time. But she returned in 1957, winning the U.S. National and her first Wimbledon title. The following year, she won both tournaments for the second time.

Then, surprisingly, at the age of thirty, Gibson retired from professional tennis and pursued other activities, to make the money that tennis, at that point, did not provide. She recorded albums, acted briefly, toured with the Harlem Globetrotters, and became a celebrity endorser.

Gibson played professional golf from 1963 to 1967 as the first Black member of the Ladies Professional Golf Association. Later she worked for the New Jersey State Athletic Control Board. She has served as special consultant to the New Jersey Governor's Council on Physical Fitness since 1988.

Jacqueline Joyner-Kersee
(1962–)
TRACK

Jacqueline Joyner-Kersee was born to teen parents in East St. Louis, Illinois, with three siblings. Her family was very poor and strict. Jackie was not allowed to date until she was eighteen. However, she was allowed to play at the recreational center across the street from her home. They wanted her to learn dance and other feminine activities but Jackie wanted to run, jump, and play ball. She ran in her first track meet, lost, and contemplated quitting. She persisted and won five first places in one day. In high school she won four consecutive National Junior Pentathlon Championships. She broke a record in her favorite event—the long jump. As a result, she made the U.S. Olympic team as a high school senior. Unfortunately, in 1980, the United States boycotted the games. Jackie also played volleyball and basketball and averaged 53 points per game. Her parents stressed education, and she graduated in the top 10 percent of her class.

Jackie's mother died in her second semester at UCLA. It was a crushing blow, but a young assistant coach named Bobby Kersee encouraged her and became her personal track coach. He helped Jackie achieve her personal best in the seven hepthalon events. Both realized she should quit basketball and pursue winning gold medals.

In 1984, she graduated from college, and both her and her brother won medals in the Olympics. Kersee hurt her hamstring, but still won a silver medal in the hepthalon. Her brother Al won a gold medal in the triple jump. Her typical workout, under the watchful eye of Bobby, began at 7:30 a.m. and did not conclude until 7:00 p.m. The day consisted of jogging, sprinting, weights, physical therapy, and reviewing past performances.

The tough training routine paid off. She won back-to-back gold medals in the Hepthalon in 1988 and 1992, a feat never before duplicated. Kersee scored more than seven thousand points in the hepthalon. This had never been done before and she did it seven times! She also won a gold and silver in the long jump. In 1996, she had to withdraw from the hepthalon, again due to injury, but she won a bronze in the long jump. She felt that was her greatest performance. Her last races were in 1998, and she again won, with the finale in her hometown area of St. Louis, Jackie is known as "the greatest female athlete of all time."

Her next challenge is to rebuild East St. Louis and become a sports agent. Her friend and coach also became her husband.

Carl Lewis

(1961–)

TRACK

Carl Lewis' parents considered their son the third best athlete in the family of four. His parents were track coaches and former athletes. His mother, Evelyn, was a world-class hurdler and represented the United States at the 1951 Pan American Games. His sister Carol was a national star in the long jump.

Carl was determined to prove his parents wrong. He went out to his backyard, marked off 29' 2," and practiced jumping this length. He made breaking the world record his personal goal. He grew up in New Jersey and competed at Willingboro High-School. He was the state champion in the 100 meters and the long jump. He was ranked the top high school track athlete in the country. Through hard work and determination, he was rewarded with a scholarship to the University of Houston.

Lewis' track accomplishments parallel those of his hero, Jesse Owens. In 1984, he won four gold medals just like Owens and in the same events—the 100, 200, 400 meter relays, and the long jump. Many feel he was the greatest track athlete of all time because he has won nine gold medals, more than any other athlete, and qualified in five Olympics. He might have qualified for six had the United States not boycotted the games in 1980. In his favorite event, the long jump, he won the gold in 1984, 1988, 1992, and 1996.

Lewis was considered the underdog in 1996 to Mike Powell, who had broken Bob Beamon's record of 29' 2". Always the competitor, King Carl once again showed his brilliance. Ironically, the American media responded better to Carl as the underdog in 1996 than when he won so brilliantly in 1984. They wanted him to show more humility, like Jesse Owens. They felt that his arrogance meant that he was concerned about money more than the love of the sport.

Lewis helped found the Santa Monica Track Club. Carl always felt misunderstood by the media, advertisers, and the public. He believed that world-class track athletes should be compensated and respected like their peers in other sports. The European public agreed, and he was well received and paid very well.

Carl retired in 1997 with a personal best of 9.78 in the 100 and 19.75 in the 200; and he reached his goal of 29.27 in the long jump.

Florence "FloJo" Griffith Joyner
(1959–1998)
TRACK

Florence Griffith Joyner was born in Los Angeles and lived in the Watts community. She was the seventh of eleven children. Her parents divorced when she was four. She was named after her mother, and to avoid confusion, was called Dee Dee.

Her mother was a seamstress and ran a tight, biblically based house. Television was replaced with Bible study and family meetings during the week, and lights were out by ten o'clock. Joyner said in a *Newsweek* interview, "Everybody in the family survived. Nobody does drugs, nobody got shot. We were afraid of Mama's voice. We didn't know how poor we were. We were rich as a family."

Joyner loved running. At the age of five, she would catch jackrabbits in the desert. At seven, she was a member of the Sugar Ray Robinson Youth Foundation track team. She excelled in high school, setting records in the sprints and long jump. Her high school rival, Valerie Brisco, beat her for the third spot on the 1980 Olympic team.

Joyner met Bobbie Kersee and was extremely impressed by his coaching ability. She changed colleges and moved to UCLA to run under his tutelage. She graduated from UCLA in 1983. Once again, she placed second in the 200 meters in the 1984 Olympics to Valerie Brisco-Hooks. Placing second took an emotional toll on Joyner.

She married Al Joyner, the 1984 Olympic triple jump winner in 1987. Al loved her dearly. He encouraged her and they trained together. Eventually, she was able to outsprint Al.

Joyner once again returned to her coach, Bobbie Kersee, with the sole objective of winning the 1988 Olympics. She had a husband and a new attitude, and became FloJo with her see-through body suits, one-legged leotards, bikini briefs, long manicured nails, and jazzy hairstyles. Some of her opponents took offense, but the media loved her.

Joyner trained four hours during the afternoon and two hours at night. She trained while working a clerical job in the morning and braiding hair in the evenings. Her effort paid off. She won three gold medals in the 100 and 200 meters and the 400-meter relay. She also won the silver in the 1600-meter relay. She broke two world records in the 100 with a time of 10.49, and the 200 in 21.34. Her opponents again showed their jealousy and accused her of using steroids. She passed eleven drug tests.

Joyner retired in 1989, to the dismay of her public, and embarked on a writing, modeling, and fashion career. She served as chair of the President's Council on Physical Fitness. She was inducted into the Track Hall of Fame in 1995.

In 1998, FloJo died of a seizure in her sleep. Once again her opponents attributed it to drugs. She passed her final drug test in an autopsy. She is survived by her husband and daughter.

Jesse Owens
(1913–1980)
TRACK

Jesse Owens was born James Cleveland Owens in rural Alabama. Owens' gift was noticed early, as he was constantly outrunning the local boys, even though he suffered from malnutrition.

Charles Riley, an amazed and sympathetic coach, took Owens under his wing. Owens worked out with Riley for forty-five minutes a day before school and worked several jobs after school. As a high school senior, he tied the world record in the 100-yard dash and won three events in the 1933 National Interscholastic Championships in Chicago. It was the first of several astonishing track meets that put Owens in the record books.

The next meet came on May 25, 1935, when Owens was a student at Ohio State University. He participated in a Big Ten Conference track meet at the University of Michigan. The twenty-one-year-old Owens tied the world record for the 100-yard dash and set new world records for the 220-yard low hurdles and the broad jump (now referred to as the long jump).

That was just the beginning. The icing on the cake came when Owens won four gold medals at the 1936 Olympic Games in Berlin, Germany, dashing Adolf Hitler's boasts of Aryan superiority, before the eyes of the entire world. Not only did he win the gold, but he tied the Olympic records for the 200-meter run and the long jump. Hitler was so disgusted that an American, let alone an *African American*, had embarrassed him in front of his country by breaking the world record for the 400-meter relay race and others, that he refused to shake his hand, though he had personally congratulated other earlier Olympic winners. He couldn't afford to finish college, and he eventually got a job as a city playground worker.

It wasn't until twenty years later, in 1955, that America recognized Owen's accomplishments. The government sent him abroad as Ambassador of Sports and he gave speeches on patriotism and fair play. He was also secretary of the Illinois State Athletic Commission.

In 1990, Owens was posthumously awarded the Congressional Medal of Honor and also appeared on a commemorative postage stamp.

Jesse Owens died in Arizona on March 31, 1980. He is survived by a wife and three daughters.

Wilma Rudolph
(1940–1994)
TRACK

Wilma Rudolph was born in Clarkesville, Tennessee, the twentieth child in a family of twenty-two. She was disabled with polio during her childhood and was told she would never walk, much less run and play basketball. God, her parents, Wilma, and Meharry Medical school believed differently. She spent almost as much time in therapy as school. She wore a brace for six years.

The therapy proved successful, and Wilma Rudolph became a basketball and track star in high school. She scored 803 points in her sophomore year, setting a school record. She was so talented that at the age of 16, she earned a spot on the Olympic team in 1956. She won a bronze medal in the 400-meter relay.

Rudolph earned a full scholarship to Tennessee State University in 1957. She excelled in track. In 1960, she became the first American woman to win three gold medals. She won the 100 meters and set the world record. She also won the 200 and anchored the 400-meter relay. In 1961, Rudolph received the Sullivan Award, which is given to the top amateur athlete in the United States, and the Female Athlete of the Year Award. Wilma was the first woman to be invited to run in the Melrose Games, Penn Relays, and the Drake Relays. She graduated from Tennessee State University in 1961.

Unfortunately, during her era there were no professional outlets for female basketball players or track athletes, regardless of gender. Rudolph remained active by coaching and teaching. She founded the Wilma Rudolph Foundation in Indianapolis to develop inner-city talent. She married her high school sweetheart, Robert Ethridge, and had two daughters.

Tragedy struck this brilliant star again when she got brain cancer. She died at the age of 54. Her autobiography, *Wilma*, was developed into a movie. Her story is an inspiration to all who value courage and tenacity.

Jim Brown
(1936–)
FOOTBALL

Born in St. Simons Island, Georgia, Jim Brown was abandoned by his mother and father. He was raised by his great-grandmother in New York. Brown has tremendous determination and would not allow his lack of parental involvement to dictate his future.

He was recruited by forty-five universities and chose Syracuse. He played football, basketball, lacrosse, and ran track. He earned ten varsity letters. He placed fifth nationwide in the decathlon and qualified for the 1956 Olympics. He was often compared to Olympian Jim Thorpe.

Jim Brown was drafted by the Cleveland Browns in 1957. He was an instant star and won Rookie of the Year award. The following year he was voted the league's Most Valuable Player award. Over the course of his nine-year career, he never missed a game. This is absolutely remarkable in a game filled with injuries.

Brown had an illustrious career. He made the Pro Bowl every year. He rushed for 126 career touchdowns. He averaged 20 carries, 104 yards, and a record-setting 5.2 yards per carry. He rushed for 12,312 yards, which was surpassed only by Walter Payton. Barry Sanders nears that figure, but both Payton and Sanders played in more games.

Jim Brown retired at the young age of thirty. In his last year, he led the league in rushing, as he did in all but one of his nine seasons. He was the league MVP in his last season. He was inducted into the Hall of Fame in 1971.

Why did Jim Brown quit when he was still the best? He could have played for a few more years and put his record into the stratosphere. The answer lies in the mystique of the man. He did not belong to the Cleveland Browns. He was not a horse to be ridden until they found another stud. He was a man with integrity, principle, and conviction. In an interview with the *Washington Post*, Brown said, "I was a highly paid over-glamorized gladiator. The decision makers are the men who own the team, not the ones who play."

He pursued an acting career and performed in 32 movies. His best performances were in *Dirty Dozen* and *Ice Station Zebra*. He became active in reducing gang violence, homicide, and drug distribution in the Black community. He formed the American I Can corporation to empower Black youth. He remains very critical of athletes who are apolitical and indifferent to the problems facing African American people.

He has three children.

Wilt Chamberlain
(1936–)
BASKETBALL

Wilt Chamberlain was born and raised in Philadelphia and grew up with nine siblings. In the early 1950s there were few basketball players. Wilt was considered the best high school basketball player in the country. He attended the University of Kansas and spent one year with the Harlem Globetrotters. He possessed a rare combination of strength, speed, and agility. He ran the 440, 880, threw the shotput, and high jumped. He received several offers to become a boxer and play tight end in football.

He was drafted by his hometown Philadelphia Warriors (later the 76'ers) in 1959 for an unprecedented $65,000. He is the only player to be Rookie of the Year and Most Valuable Player (MVP). He achieved the feat in 1959. His major nemesis was Bill Russell and the Boston Celtics. Chamberlain and the Warriors finally beat Bill Russell and the Celtics in 1967 for the championship. Chamberlain won again with the Lakers in 1972. He was a tireless athlete. He averaged 48.5 minutes per game. This resulted because of many overtime games. He literally played the entire game. He broke a record with 4,029 minutes for the entire season.

Chamberlain is probably best known for his scoring prowess. He led the league in scoring seven consecutive seasons (1960–1966). He led the league in rebounds 11 seasons (1960–1963, 1966–1968, 1971–1973). He once scored 100 points, and scored 65 points or more on 15 occasions. Chamberlain was far more than a scorer. He averaged 23 rebounds per game. He is the only center to lead the league in assists. He won the MVP award in 1960, and 1966–1968. He was an all-star 13 seasons. Wilt played 1,045 games without ever fouling out. He was inducted into the Hall of Fame in 1978.

Chamberlain's 14-year career included playing for the Golden State Warriors and the Los Angeles Lakers. The only player to score more points than Chamberlain (31,419) was Kareem Abdul Jabbar. The only player with a greater scoring average was Michael Jordan.

Kareem Abdul-Jabbar
(1947–)
BASKETBALL

Kareem Abdul-Jabbar was born Ferdinand Lewis Alcindor, Jr., in New York City. He played high school ball for Power Memorial High School. While there, he lead the Power Memorial team to a 95–6 record. Abdul-Jabbar was a highly regarded high school ballplayer as a three-time All-American. After high school, he joined one of the best college basketball teams in history, the UCLA Bruins. From 1967 to 1969, Abdul-Jabbar won three consecutive NCAA titles for the Bruins, leading them to an 88–2 record. He was also named the NCAA Tournament's Most Outstanding Player and College Player of the Year. He was drafted number one in 1969.

In 1971, while still a student, Abdul-Jabbar converted to the Muslim faith and changed his name. From 1969 to 1975, he played center for the Bucks and led his team to the NBA championship in the 1970–71 season.

During the 1975–1976 season, the 7' 1 3/8" Abdul-Jabbar was traded to the Los Angeles Lakers. While there, he won three more MVP trophies (1976, 1977, 1980), and teamed up with another MVP, Magic Johnson, to win five more NBA titles (1980, 1982, 1985, 1987, 1988). He was also named the NBA Finals MVP in 1971 and 1985. Over his career, Abdul-Jabbar won six MVP trophies and six world championships, along with nine NBA all-time records including most points, minutes, and blocks.

Abdul-Jabbar's signature trademarks are his "sky-hook" and are his goggles. And in addition to basketball, his other claim to fame is starring in the film *Airplane!* as copilot Murdock.

When he retired in 1989, he was the all-time NBA leader in points (38,387) and games played (1,560). Shortly thereafter, in 1995, Abdul-Jabbar was elected to the Hall of Fame, and in 1996, to the NBA's "50 Greatest Players of All Time" team.

He has four children.

Magic Johnson
(1959–)
BASKETBALL

Born Earvin Johnson in Lansing, Michigan, Johnson acquired the nickname "Magic" after a high school game in which he scored 36 points, grabbed 18 rebounds, and made 16 assists. Playing mostly point guard at Michigan State University, the 6'9" Johnson helped lead the Spartans to the National Collegiate Athletic Association (NCAA) finals in 1979. The Spartans defeated Indiana State and their star player, Larry Bird—later the star player of the Boston Celtics and considered Johnson's chief on-court rival during the 1980s—for the NCAA title.

Johnson left college after his sophomore year (1979) to join the Los Angeles Lakers. He helped lead the Lakers to five NBA championships (1980, 1982, 1985, 1987, 1988). In 1980, he became the first rookie to be named most valuable player (MVP) of the NBA finals; he was named NBA Finals MVP again in 1982 and 1987 and was the NBA's MVP three times (1987, 1989, 1990). He played in 12 all-star games and, at the time of his retirement, held the NBA record for assists (1992). He was the tallest guard in NBA history.

In the fall of 1991, Magic announced that he had tested positive for the virus that causes acquired immune deficiency syndrome (AIDS) and consequently was retiring from the Lakers. He became a national spokesperson for AIDS awareness and prevention, and established a foundation to promote AIDS research. His book, *What You Can Do to Avoid AIDS*, was published in 1992. After his poignant return to the 1992 NBA All-Star Game, the Lakers retired his jersey number (32). Johnson was a member of the United States basketball team that won the gold medal at the 1992 Summer Olympics in Barcelona, Spain, and served briefly on the President's Council on AIDS. He then announced his return to professional basketball, and in September 1992, signed another contract with the Lakers. In November of that year, however, he once again announced that he would retire, because of the AIDS controversy that was surrounding his return to basketball. He subsequently became a television sports commentator and continued his efforts to own part of an NBA franchise.

Late in the 1993–94 season, Johnson became head coach of the Lakers. Citing other interests and a frustration over player attitudes, he resigned his position at the conclusion of that season. He remains the vice-president.

Magic has become the consummate businessman. He has provided quality movie theaters in inner-city neighborhoods. Those cities include Los Angeles, Houston, Atlanta, New York, and the Baltimore—Washington area. More cities are scheduled. He partnered with Earl Graves from Black Enterprise to own the largest Coca Cola bottling distribution company by an African American. He is also a major shareholder in an inner-city bank in Los Angeles. He is a frequent guest on talk shows and hosted one for almost a year.

Magic is married and they have three children.

Michael Jordan
(1963–)
BASKETBALL

Michael Jordan was born in Brooklyn, New York, and was raised in Wilmington, North Carolina. He was the fourth of five children. He said that he played with his tongue sticking out because his father did the same while completing a task. He failed to make his high school basketball team as a freshman or sophomore. He cried after the second failure, practiced harder, and fortunately grew from 5'11" to 6'3" and made the team in his junior year. He became one of the most widely recruited athletes in the country and earned a full scholarship to the University of North Carolina.

Jordan played three seasons with the University of North Carolina. He made the championship winning shot as a freshman in 1982. He was selected captain of the 1984 gold-winning Olympic basketball team. He left college one year early and was drafted by the Chicago Bulls in 1984. Michael Jordan returned back to the University of North Carolina and earned his bachelor's degree in 1986.

Jordan played thirteen seasons and retired after the 1998 season. He missed one season when his father was killed. Michael wanted to pursue his dream of playing baseball. His batting average was only .202.

During the 13 seasons of his basketball career, he was named Rookie of the Year, was scoring champion ten times, selected to the All Star Team eleven times, and had the highest playoff average of 34.7 and regular season average 32.3. He played in 930 games. He scored 29,277 points, third behind Jabbar and Chamberlain. He was league MVP five times. He won gold again with the "Dream Team" in the 1992 Olympics.

Jordan was far more than a basketball player. He was charismatic, intelligent, and articulate. He did not renegotiate his underpriced salary and was rewarded with a $36 million contract in 1997. Jordan made more money off the court with endorsements and business ventures at $80 million annually. In 1993, Michael said, "When I leave the game, I'll leave on top. I don't want to leave after my feet have slowed, my hands aren't as quick, or my eyesight isn't as sharp. I want people to remember me playing exactly the kind of game I'm capable of playing right now. Nothing less." He kept his word six years later when he retired in 1999.

Michael is married with three children. He keeps busy with his endorsements, businesses, foundations, charitable causes, and golf.

Eldrick "Tiger" Woods
(1975–)
GOLFER

Tiger Woods is the son of Earl Woods, a retired lieutenant colonel in the U.S. Army, and his wife Kultida, a native of Thailand. He was nicknamed "Tiger" after a Vietnamese soldier and friend of the family. Tiger's father has been a great coach and mentor. At six months old, he was swinging a golf club, just like his father. He appeared on the *Mike Douglas Show* at age two and putted with Bob Hope. He shot 48 for nine holes at age three and was featured in Golf Digest at age five.

Woods was born in Cypress, California, which is 35 miles southeast of Los Angeles. Before turning pro he attended Stanford University for two years. Tiger has been a champion all his life. He won the Optimist International Junior Tournament at ages 8, 9, 12, 13, 14, and 15. In 1991, at age 15, he was the youngest ever to win the U.S. Junior Amateur Championship. In his two years at Stanford, he won 10 collegiate events, including the NCAA Crown with a record of 67.

Tiger wanted more challenges and turned pro in August 1996. He was the first pro to earn more than $2 million in one year. He is ranked number one in the world and shot under 64 more than 15 times.

Tiger's greatest achievement was his performance at the 1997 Masters Tournament. He was the youngest player to ever win at the tender age of 21. Moreover, he was the first African or Asian to win this prestigious tournament. He broke the record by shooting a 270, 18 strokes below par, and won with the greatest margin of victory—12 strokes. What is next for the Tiger?

Pelé
(1940–)
SOCCER

Pelé was born Edson Arantes do Nascimento in a small village called Três Corações in the Brazilian state of Minas Gerais. His father, João Ramos do Nascimento, or Dondinho, as he was known in the soccer world, was a professional player. He was well known as one of the best heading players in his time. He was a center forward for Fluminense until an injury kept him from playing professional division one soccer. When he was a child, Pele and his family moved to Baurú, in the interior of the Braziliam state of São Paulo. There he learned to master the sport of *futebol*.

Pelé's soccer career started early. At the age of eleven, he was discovered by a former Brazilian World Cup player named Waldemar de Brito. De Brito recognized Pelé's skills and invited him to join the team he was organizing. In 1956, when he was fifteen, Pelé went to São Paulo to try out for the professional club called Santos Futebol Clube (SFC).

Not long after his first season with the SFC, Sylvio Pirilo, Brazil's national coach at the time, called Pelé to his squad. When he was sixteen, he played for the Brazilian national team against Argentina's squad and scored the one goal for Brazil in their 2–1 loss. In 1961, he was given the nickname "The King" by the French press when he played a few matches in Europe.

In the late 1960s, when he and his team, Santos, went to Nigeria to play a few friendly matches, the ongoing civil war stopped for the duration of his visit. A 48-hour armistice was signed with Biafra so that both sides could go and watch Pelé play a round of exhibition matches. Two hundred thousand people attended the matches.

Pelé became the only player to participate in three World Cup victories when he led the Brazilian national team to titles in 1958 (Sweden), 1962 (Chile), 1966 (England), and 1970 (Mexico); he scored 12 goals in 14 World Cup matches. In 1959, he established the Paulist league goal-scoring record for one season—126 goals. In 1969, he scored his famous 1,000th goal from a penalty kick in the 34th minute of the game against Vasco da Gama, and dedicated it "para as criancinhas pobres do Brasil" (to the poor little children of Brazil) and to the elderly and suffering peoples of Brazil. Pelé also participated in what is known as the "Golden Age" of the Libertadores Cup from 1960 to 1963, during which the great Uruguayan team, Penarol, faced the legendary Santos for the final games.

By 1974, when he retired for the first time, Pelé had scored 1,283 goals in 1,363 professional games and had become a Brazilian national hero. From 1975 to 1977, he came out of retirement to play with the New York Cosmos of the North American Soccer League, leading them to a league championship in 1977. Pelé's contract with the Cosmos made him the highest-paid athlete in the world at the time. He is credited with popularizing soccer in the United States. After his subsequent retirement in 1977, he became an international ambassador for the sport, working to promote peace and understanding through friendly athlete competition.

Isaac Murphy
(1861–1896)
JOCKEY

Isaac Murphy was born Isaac Burns, a slave in Lexington, Kentucky, possibly on January 1 (the birth date given for all thoroughbred horses), 1861. After the death of his father, a Union soldier in the Civil War, and the issuance of the Emancipation Proclamation, he moved with his family to the farm of his maternal grandfather, Green Murphy, and took his surname.

When Murphy was twelve years old, his family added two years to his age so that he could get an apprentice jockey's license. In May 1875, he ran his first race, in Louisville, Kentucky, but didn't win a meet until sixteen months later. That first win sparked an unparalleled string of successes.

Murphy became the first jockey to win the Kentucky Derby three times (1884, 1890, and 1891)—a feat unsurpassed for 57 years—and the first to win back-to-back Derbys. He also won four of the first five runnings of the American Derby at Washington Park in Chicago (1884 to 1886, and 1888). In 1882, he ran a string of forty-nine incredible victories in fifty-one starts at Saratoga Downs in New York.

During his career, Murphy won 44 percent of his races—that's 628 races that he won out of 1,412 mounts. It was said that Murphy knew how to pace a horse better than anyone in the sport of racing. He rode with only his hands and heels and only used the whip to satisfy the crowd. Newspapers and trainers of the day referred to him as the greatest jockey. Like most of the young riders of his time, he virtually lived and slept at the track. He became proficient in the art of hand-riding, which made him more in tune with his mount. Legend had it that a horse could jump straight up and down, but Murphy would never rise off his back.

Noted for his integrity, honesty, honor, and character, Murphy became the undisputed king of his profession, which at that time had the largest spectator attendance in America. By 1882, he earned $10,000 a year for salary. By the end of his career, it was estimated that he earned $250,000 a year.

Murphy was the head-to-head winner of one of the most publicized races of the late nineteenth century. Settling a debate over whether he could defeat the best White jockey of that time, Snapper Garrison, they raced and Murphy emerged from the race, victorious.

Unfortunately, in 1891, following his third Derby victory, Murphy's career ended. He was prone to putting on weight during the off-season and would balloon up to 140 pounds or more during the winter. Then he would diet during the spring races. This unhealthy practice eventually weakened his body and he became prone to infection. On February 12, 1896, Isaac Murphy died of pneumonia at the age of 35.

In 1955, he was the first rider voted to the Jockey Hall of Fame.

Joe Louis
(1914–1981)
BOXER

Joe Louis was born Joe Louis Barrow in 1914 at the beginning of World War I to Alabama share-croppers. With visions of her son becoming a great violinist, Louis' mother decided to move the family to Detroit, Michigan, when he was twelve years old. After a few lessons, however, he decided to quit.

In 1932, a friend, who was also the Golden Gloves champion that year, invited Louis to work out with him as his sparring partner. When a right punch almost knocked his friend out of the ring, Louis knew he had found his calling.

In 1935, after an amazing string of victories, Louis finally faced a major opponent—former world heavyweight champion Primo Carnera, an Italian. To many, Carnera represented the fascist ambitions of Benito Mussolini, the Italian dictator who was on the verge of invading Ethiopia. Louis was an African American who symbolized the free world and also the pride of the African people. The night of the fight, Yankee stadium was filled with African and Italian Americans. In the sixth round, the Italian Stallion was defeated by the Brown Bomber.

In June 1936, Louis faced another major opponent, this time the symbol of Aryan supremacy, Max Schmeling, the German former heavyweight champion. Unfortunately, in the twelfth round, the Brown Bomber was knocked out. But in 1937, he came back to recapture the title from James J. Braddock with an eighth-round knockout. In 1938, he faced Schmeling again for a rematch, which got international atten-tion. In what some have described as the most anticipated fight of the century, Louis avenged himself and his race with an amazing first-round knockout in two minutes and four seconds. Millions of Black radio listeners cheered in delight at the news of Louis' victory. Morale was lifted for many during the bleak year of the Great Depression. In Harlem, tens of thousands chanted in the streets, "Joe Louis is the first Ameri-can to KO a Nazi."

Louis went on to defend his title twenty-five times. He became known as the first African Ameri-can hero. He destroyed the myth of racial inferiority as he defeated his opponents time and again in the ring. Known as the greatest prizefighter this country has ever known, the Brown Bomber died April 12, 1981, in Las Vegas, Nevada.

He is survived by a wife and two children.

Jack Johnson
(1878–1946)
BOXER

Jack Johnson was born John Arthur Johnson in Galveston, Texas. He quit school in the fifth grade to work. He got several odd jobs, including longshoring on the city's docks, which helped build his muscle strength. Despite the objections of his parents, he began training as a boxer. In 1897, at the age of nineteen, he began boxing professionally. He stood more than 6 feet tall and weighed 180 lbs.

By 1901, Johnson had become the best boxer in Texas and began boxing successfully across the country. In 1903, after winning the Negro heavyweight championship, he demanded to fight Jim Jeffries, the reigning White champion. Jeffries decided to retire from boxing rather than demean himself by fighting a Black man, though later he did fight Johnson.

In 1908, Canadian fighter Tommy Burns won the vacated title, and fought Johnson. For thirteen rounds, Johnson kept up a running conversation with Burns, even though he was beating him. Bloodied and nearly broken, Burns refused to quit. Finally, in the fourteenth round, the police were called in to stop the fight. The new champion became an instant hero to Black America and a despised foe for White America, whose boasts of superiority over Blacks in all areas were shattered.

Johnson fanned the flames even more by being an arrogant figure in the ring and out. He swaggered, wore flashy clothes and jewelry, had six cars and a large entourage, and openly bragged about romancing and marrying White women. As a result, the boxing community came up with a succession of "Great White Hopes" to try and dethrone this "uppity" Black fighter.

After Burns' humiliation, Jeffries was lured out of retirement as the White hope to defeat Johnson. Johnson's fifteenth-round knockout of Jeffries in 1910 led to several deadly race riots across the country.

In 1913, Johnson was convicted of violating the Mann Act for transporting his girlfriend, later his wife, across state lines for unlawful purposes, for which he was sentenced to one year in jail. He and his wife fled to Canada and then to France.

Johnson defended his title until 1915, when he lost it in a twenty-sixth-round knockout by Jess Willard in Cuba. There is still some controversy regarding the outcome of the fight; there is speculation that Johnson threw the fight, hoping that the government would drop the charges against him.

Johnson fought professionally from 1897 to 1928, and boxed in exhibitions around the world as late as 1945. In those forty-eight years in the ring, he fought 114 bouts and was knocked out only three times. On June 10, 1946, Jack Johnson's flamboyant life-style ended when he died in an automobile accident.

Muhammad Ali
(1942–)
BOXER

Muhammad Ali was born Cassius Marcellus Clay, Jr., in Louisville, Kentucky. As an amateur boxer in 1960 by winning the Amateur Athletic Union light heavyweight and Golden Gloves heavyweight championships. He won a gold medal in the light heavyweight division at the 1960 Olympic Games in Rome. He turned professional soon afterward and became the world heavyweight champion after knocking out Sonny Liston in seven rounds on February 25, 1964.

Ali successfully defended his title nine times from 1965 to 1967 and was universally recognized as champion after defeating World Boxing Association (WBA) champion Ernie Terrell. Ali often proclaimed his invincibility by boasting "I am the greatest" his personal slogan.

In 1964, he joined the Nation of Islam (Black Muslims) and adopted the Muslim name Muhammad Ali. In 1967, he refused to be inducted into the United States Army on the grounds that he was a Black Muslim minister and therefore a conscientious objector. He was subsequently convicted of violating the Selective Service Act, and the ruling bodies of boxing declared his title vacant. Ali returned to the ring in 1970. Later that year the U.S. Supreme Court overturned his conviction. He won title fights against Joe Frazier and George Foreman. Ali regained the WBA title from Spinks becoming the first boxer ever to win the championship three times.

In 1979, Ali announced his retirement, at that point having lost only three decisions in 59 fights. He returned to fight World Boxing Council Champion Larry Holmes in 1980 and Trevor Berbick of Canada in 1981, but lost both fights. In 1984, it was confirmed that Ali was suffering from Parkinson disease.

In 1996, he was selected to carry the torch and light the flame at the Olympic Games in Atlanta. He is married with nine children.

Eddie Robinson

(1919–)

FOOTBALL COACH

Eddie Robinson was born in Jackson, Louisiana, the son of a sharecropping family. He was a gifted quarterback and earned a scholarship to Leland College in Baker, Louisiana. He graduated from college, but during the Jim Crow era there were few professional opportunities in sports. His desire was to coach, but White schools would not consider him, and Black schools were well staffed. He took a job at a feed mill for 25 cents an hour.

In 1941, he applied for a coaching position at Louisiana Negro Normal and Industrial Institute—now Grambling State University. He heard they were looking for a coach. Robinson accepted the position realizing that he would be the offensive, defensive, and special team's coach. No coach has won more games and championships and sent more players to the NFL and the Hall of Fame.

Over a 57-year career, Robinson, won 402 games, breaking the old record by legendary Bear Bryant at the University of Alabama. Robinson placed more than 200 players in the NFL, including Hall of Famers Willie Brown, Willie Davis, and Buck Buchanan. The first Black quarterback to play in the Super Bowl game was his former player, Doug Williams. Doug went on to be named Most Valuable Player of the game. Robinson told the *Detroit Free Press,* "For years I wanted desperately to find out what it would take to get a Grambling player to be an NFL quarterback. I went to every NFL scout I knew. We ran our offenses like pro teams. I never accepted the fact that there could not be a Black quarterback, coach, or owner. Anything is possible in our society if people are willing to pay the price."

Coaching was never work to him because he enjoyed it so much. His day would begin at 6:30 a.m. and often would not end until midnight. He is the only coach of a Black college to have graced the cover of *Sports Illustrated.* He is married with one child. Robinson retired in 1997, and Doug Williams took over the helm.

ENTERTAINMENT

IX

Quincy Jones
(1933–)
PRODUCER

Quincy Jones was born in Chicago. His early role models were Charlie Parker and Ray Charles. He started playing the trumpet at age fifteen and studied music on scholarship at Boston's prestigious Berklee College of Music in 1951. He played in Lionel Hampton's and Dizzie Gillespie's bands in the late 1950s.

Quincy, also known as "Q," has always been willing to take risks with his music. He has explored many forms of music and is not afraid to create fusion between them. This multitalented musician has written for hundreds of artists, including Michael Jackson, Count Basie, Frank Sinatra, Sarah Vaughan, Tevin Campbell, Winans, and many rappers.

He has won more than thirty Grammy awards and has been nominated for seventy-six, including Michael Jackson's album *Off the Wall*, which sold eight million copies, and *Thriller*, which sold more than 46 million units. He is a sought-after soundtrack composer, with more than fifty movies to his credit, including *In the Heat of the Night, Bob and Carol and Ted and Alice, The Wiz, Roots*, and *The Color Purple*. The latter film won eleven Oscar nominations.

The gifted musician is also a great humanitarian. He collaborated with Michael Jackson, Diana Ross, Lionel Ritchie, and Stevie Wonder to produce the charity single, *We Are the World*, which raised $50 million in 1991.

The consummate businessman, he created his own label Qwest. His album *Back on the Block*, featuring many stars, won six Grammy awards. He is the founder of *Vibe magazine*, which features cutting edge trends in the Black music industry. He produced *Fresh Prince of Bel-Air* and the *Jenny Jones* show.

His music spans five decades and he remains the genius of the industry. He is married with five children.

Suzanne de Passe
(1948–)

PRODUCER

Suzanne de Passe was born in Harlem, New York, to West Indian parents. She attended the prestigious New Lincoln High School. She majored in English at Manhattan Community College and Syracuse University.

de Passe began her career as a talent coordinator for a popular Manhattan discotheque. She was also a talent consultant for Howard Stein. While she was there, Cindy Birdsong of the Supremes introduced her to Berry Gordy of Motown. In 1968, Gordy offered her a position as creative assistant. She advanced in the company and became director of the West Coast operation. Later she became president of Motown Records.

de Passe worked with the Jacksons, Michael Jackson, Smokey Robinson, Stevie Wonder, Lionel Ritchie, Stephanie Mills, Rick James, the Temptations, the Commodores, and many more. She wrote and produced Diana Ross' television special and "Going Back to Indiana" featuring the Jacksons in 1970. In 1972, she wrote and produced *Lady Sings the Blues*. She was involved in producing, *The Wiz*. Suzanne produced Berry Gordy's movie *The Last Dragon* and *Motown 25, Motown 30,* and *Motown 40* television specials.

She was executive producer for *Lonesome Dove* and *Sister Sister*. She won Emmys for *Lonesome Dove* and *Motown Returns to the Apollo*. In 1990, Suzanne was inducted into the Black Filmmakers Hall of Fame.

Suzanne de Passe left Motown in 1988 and gained national attention when she established her own company, de Passe Entertainment, in 1992. She also produced two television movies, *Callie and Son* and an afterschool special, *Out of Step*. Suzanne developed two theater works, *Satchmo,* a biography of Louis Armstrong, and *Daddy Goodness*.

Don Cornelius

(1936–)

PRODUCER

Don Cornelius was born and raised in Chicago. People often remarked about his beautiful and distinctive voice. Cornelius paid $400 and took a broadcasting course. He landed a job on WVON in Chicago as a part-time announcer. His mentor, Roy Wood, moved to WCIU-TV and Cornelius followed.

Cornelius wanted to provide a Black alternative to Dick Clark and *American Bandstand.* The format would feature teen dancers and popular Black artists. WCIU agreed, but the problem would be securing a sponsor. Finally George O'Hare, an officer from Sears, secured assistance. On August 17, 1970, *Soul Train* premiered. Cornelius wrote, hosted, produced, and sold advertising. *Soul Train* became the number 1 show for African Americans in Chicago.

Cornelius felt that since the show was successful in Chicago, it should receive similar ratings nationally. Again, the challenge would be securing a sponsor. George Johnson of Johnson Haircare Products filled the void. It was a perfect marriage between his products and a young Black audience. *Soul Train* went national on October 2, 1971. The success did not go unnoticed by Dick Clark. Clark recruited *Soul Train* dancers for his own Black dance show called *Soul Unlimited,* which was backed by the powerful ABC-TV network. Cornelius and Clark met and resolved their differences and produced some specials together.

In 1975, Cornelius collaborated with Dick Griffiy and formed *Soul Train* records. This venture experienced moderate success. It folded in 1978. In 1986, Cornelius established the Soul Train Music Awards, the first and, at that time, only music awards dedicated exclusively to acknowledge the achievements of Black Americans.

By 1992, *Soul Train* was the longest-running music program in the history of syndication. Cornelius remains the executive producer, but now he has others to write, host, and sell advertising. He is married with two sons.

Kenneth "Baby Face" Edmonds
(1959–)
PRODUCER AND SINGER

Baby Face Edmonds was born in Indianapolis and found creative ways to interview top musical stars about their craft. He learned to play the guitar and keyboards in elementary school. While playing in a band after high school, he hooked up with L.A. Reid, and they began producing for Dick Griffey and Solar Records. They wrote and produced for the Whispers, Shalamar, Karyn White, and After 7.

In 1989, Edmonds and Reid formed their own label, LaFace, and wrote and produced for Paula Abdul, Whitney Houston, Sheena Easton, and others. Edmonds also became a solo artist, swooning his audience with his voice and his writing.

Kenneth Edmonds is a very modest, humble, and multitalented young man. He will tell you he is a fair keyboard player, with a below-average voice, who just happened to luck into producing. Tell that to Michael Jackson, Toni Braxton, Aretha Franklin, Whitney Houston, Boyz II Men, Mariah Carey, Vanessa Williams, TLC, Madonna, and numerous others who all have sung his music.

His production skills are not confined to the recording studio. He has been very successful producing sound tracks for movies like *Boomerang* and *Waiting to Exhale*. Both sound tracks went platinum and won many Grammy awards for Baby Face. He has produced seventy-five top ten R&B and pop hits. He has thirty-three songs that went number 1. In 1997 he tied the record with twelve Grammy nominations. He has won more than forty throughout his career.

He and his wife Tracey, who is a movie producer, are the talk of Beverly Hills. They collaborated in the production of the movie *Soul Food*. They have one child.

Josephine Baker
(1906–1975)
ENTERTAINER

On June 3, 1906, Josephine Carson was born in St. Louis, Missouri, the first child of a drummer and a maid. At the tender age of eight, Baker herself began to work as a domestic like her mother. By the age of fourteen, Baker had left her parents home, gotten married and gotten separated from her new husband. While waitressing to earn her living, Baker developed a keen interest in the entertainment business. She joined a band of street performers called the Jones Family. When the group joined a traveling show called the Dixie Fliers, young Josephine was on the road.

Baker practiced her skills as a dancer and made comedy a part of her routine. One of Baker's many trademarks was to perform a complicated series of dance steps while keeping her eyes crossed. Her chance to work for a major production finally came in 1924 when she joined the cast of Noble Sissle and Eubie Blake's *Chocolate Dandies*. After the show ended, Baker's work at the Plantation Club landed her her first big break. A wealthy woman from Chicago who was a great fan of black musicals decided to create a show that would tour Paris. Filling a role originally intended for (blues singer) Ethel Waters, the skillful Josephine negotiated her salary from $125 to $200 per week which was a small fortune for that time. Baker was on her way to France as a member of *La Revue Negre*.

Baker was met with general adoration and fascination by the people in the city that she would learn to call home. Not only did she entertain the French people, she also became a national hero.

During the '50s and '60s she protested on behalf of civil rights in the United States. The National Association for the Advancement of Colored People declared May 20, 1951 "Josephine Baker Day" and declared her the "Most Outstanding Woman of the Year." In 1963, Baker participated in the March on Washington and also gave a benefit performance for several civil rights organizations.

Unable to have children of her own, Baker created what she called her "Rainbow Tribe" when she adopted twelve children of many different nationalities who lived with her in her private community called Les Milandes.

Her career stretched more than fifty years. Josephine Baker died of a stroke on April 12, 1975 just four days after the opening of a successful show (depicting) her life story. Twenty thousand people attended her funeral which was broadcast on French national television. She is the only American woman to be honored by the French government with a twenty-one-gun salute.

Sammy Davis, Jr.
(1925–1990)
ENTERTAINER

Sammy Davis, Jr., was born in Harlem, New York to show business parents. Davis was a tireless, multi-talented performer; he could dance, sing, and act. In one period of his career, he performed in *Golden Boy* on Broadway, which earned him a Tony nomination. He had his own television show, and he was in the movie *A Man Called Adam*. All three were on the same day. His movie was released on the same day of his morning television show. He performed on stage that evening.

Davis was a dancer who specialized in tap. He and Fred Astaire were often compared. He was also a singer. He was best known for his 1972 song "Candy Man," which was number 1 for one month. He was a member of what was affectionately known as the "Rat Pack." These great entertainers included Frank Sinatra, Dean Martin, Peter Lawford, and Joey Bishop. Sammy's presence integrated the group, and despite his fame, he was still subjected to Jim Crow. Although this was an integrated group, Sammy was often reminded of Jim Crow. He loved performing for the military, but hated that he had to perform one show for African Americans and one for Whites.

Davis enjoyed direct contact with his audiences. He performed at more than 100 clubs annually. He enjoyed performing on Broadway more than Hollywood or television.

In 1954, Sammy was in a very serious car accident which cost him his left eye. From then on, he covered it with a black patch. Although Davis was a great entertainer, his political decisions were often questioned in the Black community. The infamous picture of him hugging Richard Nixon remains in the minds of many. Davis died of lung cancer in 1990.

He is survived by a wife and four children. Three of their children were adopted.

Lena Horne
(1917–)
ENTERTAINER

Lena Horne was born in Brooklyn, New York. Her father deserted the family when she was three, and her mother left shortly thereafter. Lena's grandparents raised her. She dropped out of school and began singing in clubs. She was beautiful and possessed a lovely voice.

Her big break came at age sixteen when Cab Calloway noticed her. He took her under his wing, and they performed at the Cotton Club. Horne's career was also blessed by working with Duke Ellington, Billy Strayhorn, and Harry Belafonte. Horne was able to command $10,000 per week at the apex of her career.

Horne had a tremendous desire to act in Hollywood. The only roles reserved for Black woman were mammies. She wanted to be a star, not a maid. Horne also had to deal with resentment from Black women who felt she received better parts due to her fair skin.

Her film credits include *Black Birds of 1939; Duke Is Tops; Cabin in the Sky; Death of a Gunfighter; Lady Sings the Blues; That's Entertainment; Till the Clouds Roll By; The Wiz*, and *Stormy Weather*. The latter title is also her signature song.

In 1981, she performed nationwide to sold out audiences, *The Lady and Her Music*. The production is a culmination of her six decades of stellar entertainment and won a Tony award. She has two children.

Ray Charles
(1930–)
ENTERTAINER

Ray Charles was born in Albany, Georgia. His vision problems began at the age of three, and unfortunately, his sight deteriorated into blindness at the age of seven. He attended St. Augustine school for the blind in Florida. Blindness did not stop him; he became a professional musician at the age of eighteen.

Charles is a multi-talented musician who has not allowed the media to pigeonhole him into one brand of music. Ray loves jazz, blues, and R&B. His first album was *Baby Let Me Hold Your Hand*, in 1958. He played in Carnegie Hall in New York in 1960. In 1962, he built his own recording studio, RPM International in Los Angeles. He was an active supporter of Martin Luther King, Jr. Since then he has released *Georgia On My Mind; Hit the Road Jack; Unchain My Heart; What I'd Say; I Can't Stop Loving You,* and many more. He has won twelve Grammys during his illustrious career.

Hollywood and Madison Avenue have also been blessed by the genius of Ray Charles. He has appeared in more than twenty films. He earns almost as much from endorsements as from albums. His most popular commercial is for Diet Pepsi in which he sings, "You got the right one baby."

Charles has been inducted into the Rock and Roll, Jazz, and Rhythm and Blues Halls of Fame.

Debbie Allen
(1950–)
ENTERTAINER

Debbie Allen was born in Houston, and she and her sister Phylicia Rashad have been dazzling audiences since childhood. Allen earned a bachelor's degree in fine arts from Howard University in 1971. Howard also bestowed her an honorary doctorate degree. She also earned a degree from North Carolina School of the Arts.

Allen is multi-talented, as demonstrated by her gifts as a dancer, choreographer, actor, director, and producer. She mastered her craft in dance and choreography under the tutelage of Alvin Ailey and Katherine Dunham. She has performed on Broadway, Hollywood, and television. She has earned two Tony nominations for her Broadway performances in *West Side Story* (1980) and *Sweet Charity* (1986). She also received the Drama Desk Award for the former play.

She acted in *Roots, JoJo Dancer, Ragtime, Your Life Is Coming,* and *Fish That Saved Pittsburgh,* among others. Allen choreographed the Academy Awards for a record-setting six years (1991–1995, 1999).

Allen is a highly sought after director. She directed *Fame* to two Emmys. Her resumé also includes *Different World; Family Ties; Out of Sync;, Quantum Leap; Polly, Polly Come Home; Stompin at the Savoy;* and many others.

Allen is extremely intense and passionate about her beliefs. After reading about Joseph Cinque and the Amistad, she set out on a mission to bring the story to Hollywood. Hollywood resisted for thirteen years, but Allen's persistence prevailed. She finally produced the movie in 1998. It received worldwide acclaim and it was nominated for an Oscar.

As much as Allen enjoys her profession, her pride and joy is her husband, Norm Nixon, the former basketball star, and their two beautiful children.

Oscar Micheaux
(1884–1951)

DIRECTOR

Oscar Micheaux was born January 2, 1884, in rural Cairo, Illinois, one of thirteen children of former slave parents. When he was seventeen years old, he left home to become a Pullman porter. While working the Chicago-to-Portland route, Micheaux became enchanted with life out West. In 1904, he purchased a homestead in South Dakota and became a successful farmer.

To spread the word to city-dwelling Blacks back East about the opportunities in the West, he began writing novels based on his own experiences. To sell his books, he went on promotional tours, barnstorming through the Black communities in the South and West, holding meetings in churches, schools, and homes, selling directly to the clientele.

In 1918, a Black independent film company approached him about the film rights for his novel *The Homesteader*. Micheaux insisted on directing. When they refused, he refused. He then decided to raise funds from the same people to whom he sold his books and finance his movie production. This sparked the beginning of Micheaux's career in filmmaking.

Micheaux's filmmaking style was resourceful, to say the least. He operated on shoestring budgets and shot scenes only once, leaving in whatever miscues happened to be caught on camera. He even used mirrors to enhance whatever natural lighting happened to be available. Micheaux would go on promotional tours, from town to town, stirring up demand to see his current films and to finance his future ones.

Most of Micheaux's films were melodramas, Westerns, and crime films, and these all-Black productions were far more advanced in accurately portraying lifestyles of African Americans than the Hollywood mainstream movies that portrayed Blacks in subservient and in demeaning roles.

Despite his affinity for genre movies, Micheaux attempted to address some serious issues in a few of his features. *Within Our Gates* contains a scene in which a character gets lynched; *God's Stepchildren* concerns a young light-skinned Black who tries to pass for White.

No matter the conventions of his movies, Micheaux's films always set out to do what they were supposed to do: entertain. Millions of Blacks patronized his movies in the segregated theaters of that time. Even Whites would catch midnight showings of his films.

Micheaux may not have been the most gifted filmmaker in history, but he was as big a hustler as any mainstream Hollywood producer. As one of the first and certainly most determined of African American filmmakers, he had a career that spanned thirty years, from 1918 to 1948. And in that time, he independently wrote, produced, directed, and distributed forty-eight silent and sound feature films, including *The Exile* (1931), the first all-sound film produced by a Black company; and *The Betrayal* (1948), the first African American film to premiere on Broadway. *Body and Soul* (1925) was considered by critics to be his best film; it featured Paul Robeson in his film debut.

Appropriately enough, while on a promotional tour, Oscar Micheaux died on April 1, 1951.

Spike Lee
(1957–)

DIRECTOR

Spike Lee was born Shelton Jackson Lee on March 20, 1957, in Atlanta, Georgia. He was given the nickname "Spike" by his late mother, Jacquelyn. Lee grew up in Brooklyn, New York. His early interest in the arts was stimulated by his father, Bill Lee, a noted jazz musician, and by his mother, who took him to plays, museums, and galleries.

As a student at Morehouse College in Atlanta, he pursued his interest in filmmaking. Upon graduation in 1979, he landed a summer internship at Columbia Pictures. He entered New York University's Film School, where he developed for his master's thesis *Joe's Bed-Stuy Barbershop: We Cut Heads,* an hour-long comedy about a Brooklyn barbershop involved in the local numbers' racket.

In 1982, the film won a student Academy Award from the Academy of Motion Picture Arts and Sciences, and was received with critical acclaim from San Francisco to Switzerland. However, with no offers from the Hollywood film industry to further his budding career, Lee decided to produce his works independently.

Four years later, he completed *She's Gotta Have It,* a story about the love life of a young independent Black woman. It was shot in twelve days in a small Brooklyn apartment and nearby park. It had a budget of $175,000 but went on to gross $7 million. Lee won the prize for best new film at the Cannes International Film Festival and received the Los Angeles Film Critics Award for best new director in 1986. In addition, he was named to many critics' top ten lists.

Columbia pictures picked up Lee's second film, *School Daze,* a musical about life at a Black college, for $6 million. The film made Variety's weekly list of the top ten moneymaking films in 1988.

Lee's reputation as a bona fide filmmaker blossomed after the release of his third film, *Do the Right Thing,* a story about racial tensions between Italian Americans and African Americans one hot summer day. It was a mainstream hit, and it got Lee an Academy Award nomination for best original screenplay.

Lee's controversial films continue to make box office magic. His other credits include *Mo' Better Blues, Jungle Fever, Malcolm X, Crooklyn, Clockers, Tales from the 'Hood* (he was executive producer), *Girl 6, Get on the Bus!,* and *He Got Game* as well as many television commercials. Lee's next project in the works is his second biographical epic of a famous African American, baseball's Jackie Robinson.

Spike developed a company, 40 Acres and a Mule, to distribute his products. He is married.

Jackie "Moms" Mabley

(1894–1975)

COMEDIAN

Moms Mabley was America's first (and for many years, the *only*) nationally known African American comedian. For nearly 50 years, Mabley tickled Black audiences on the so-called chitlin circuit (a national network of Black establishments) before she was discovered by the rest of the country in the 1960s. Her best-known character is a quick-witted old lady with a preference for younger men. Despite a life of tragedy and hardship, Mabley was the consummate clown who brought laughter to the lives of her audiences.

Jackie "Moms" Mabley was born Loretta Mary Aiken in Brevard, North Carolina. Aiken had eleven brothers and sisters. When she was young, her father died in an auto accident. A victim of two rapes, Aiken was the mother of two children by the time she was 14.

The young unwed mother longed for a better life for herself and her children. She left her little ones in the care of some family friends and decided to try her luck in Cleveland. In Cleveland, Mabley was in close contact with people who worked in show business. Aiken met performer Bonnie Bell Drew who took Aiken to Pittsburgh.

Aiken began to develop her own act, which included singing, dancing, and what would become her claim to fame, comedy. Aiken also met fellow performer Jack Mabley. Loretta Aiken became Jackie Mabley. Soon after she was pregnant with her third child.

The Mableys traveled the country as entertainers. They didn't make a lot of money, but they were together and they were doing what came naturally to them. It appeared that Jackie's life was taking a turn for the better.

Other areas of Mabley's life, however, were not as stable. The woman who was taking care of her two young children ran away with them and left no forwarding address. Mabley would not see her two oldest children until many years later, when they were adults. During that same time, Mabley's mother, like her father, was killed in an auto accident on Christmas Day.

Despite her personal tragedies, Mabley continued to perfect her routine. It was at this time that she developed her trademark character. Mabley began to appear onstage in shabby, oversized clothes, droopy stockings, and an old hat. In time, Nature enhanced Mabley's old lady character when she began to lose her teeth. When she became a regular performer at the Cotton Club in Harlem in the mid-1920s, fellow entertainers Louis Armstrong and Duke Ellington gave her the nickname "Moms," because Mabley often concerned herself with the welfare of other people.

Mabley had a relatively steady career working on the chitlin circuit. In the 1960s, her popularity grew when her comic recordings with Chess Records introduced her to White audiences. Mabley remained a performer up until her death in 1975.

Bill Cosby

(1937–)

COMEDIAN

Bill Cosby, America's favorite dad, was born in Philadelphia. His entertainment career began in his hometown in 1961 at the Cellar coffeehouse, where Cosby tended bar and told jokes for five dollars a night. He performed in clubs in Philadelphia and earned $60 a week. Cosby attended Temple University on a track scholarship in 1961. Just as he had dropped out of high school due to boredom, he did the same at Temple. He became a full-time comedian.

Cosby appeared several times on the *Tonight Show* starring Johnny Carson. Unlike Red Foxx or Slappy White, who performed X-rated material exclusively geared toward Black audiences, Cosby had G-rated material for everyone. He was selected as the first African American to play in a dramatic television show in 1965 with Robert Culp in *I Spy*. He won three Emmys during its successful three-year stint.

Cosby's career floundered with *The Bill Cosby Show,* his first film, *Hicky and Goggs,* and *The New Bill Cosby Show*. His unlikely success was his cartoon *Fat Albert and the Cosby Kids*. The show remained successful from 1972–1984. He teamed up with his friend Sidney Poitier in two successful comedy movies, *Uptown Saturday Night* (1974) and *Let's Do It Again* (1975).

Throughout his career, Cosby did not forget the value of education. He completed his undergraduate degree at Temple and earned his doctorate from the University of Massachusetts in 1977. His 242-page dissertation was "An Integration of the Visual Media via Fat Albert and the Cosby Kids into the Elementary School Curriculum as a Teaching Aid and Vehicle to Achieve Increased Learning."

Cosby was also concerned about the economics of his profession. He wanted to become more than a spokesman for Coca Cola, Jell-O, Kodak, Del Monte, Ford Motor Company, and the other companies he pitched. Cosby bought stock in these companies.

His major coup was his proposal to NBC for a weekly family show portraying a successful African American family. He demanded a lucrative salary and equal profit participation. The network agreed. *The Cosby Show* was a huge success among all families and reached Super Bowl proportions. There were 80 million regular viewers at its zenith. By 1992, total syndication for the show reached $1 billion, of which Cosby received $333 million. Since 1964, Bill and his wife Camille have become active philanthropists, with one contribution to Spelman alone for $20 million, the largest gift ever made to a Black college.

Cosby has written more than a dozen books, including *Fatherhood; Time Flies; Love and Marriage; Childhood; Little Bill Children Series; and Kids Say the Darndest Things,* among others. He remains on television and would like to buy a network. He and Camille were blessed with five children, but tragically lost their only son in an armed robbery. Their son was pursuing a Ph.D. before he died.

Eddie Murphy

(1961–)

COMEDIAN AND ACTOR

Eddie was born in Brooklyn, New York. His father was an amateur comedian and police officer. Murphy began working on comedy routines in elementary school. He hosted a high school talent show and did an impersonation of soul singer Al Green and was a big hit. Murphy declared in his yearbook his desire to be a comedian.

Eddie performed in clubs making $25-$50 per week. When Eddie learned that the producers of *Saturday Night Live* were looking for a Black cast member he jumped at the opportunity. He auditioned six times before winning a spot. Murphy emerged as the star of the show. He was nominated for an Emmy and a Grammy for best comedy album which went gold.

In 1982, he starred in his film, *48 Hours*. The movie was a blockbuster and Hollywood realized there was something special about Eddie Murphy. He recorded his second album, *Eddie Murphy: Comedian*. This time he won a Grammy and the album again went gold. Hollywood signed him to a $25 million contract for six films.

His next films included *Trading Places, Best Defense,* and *Beverly Hills Cop.* The latter film reached the number nine position on the all-time box-office hits.

Murphy's film credits include *Golden Child, Beverly Hills Cop II, Coming to America, Raw, Harlem Nights, Boomerang, Distinguished Gentlemen, Another 48 Hours, Vampire in Brooklyn, Nutty Professor, Metro, Doctor Doolittle,* and *Life*. His films have grossed more than $2 billion.

His television series the *PJs* has been financially successful, but has stirred controversy in the African American community for perpetuating stereotypes. At the 1988 Academy Awards, Murphy went public questioning the group for only awarding three Oscars to African American actors in its 60-year history. Eddie's mentors include the legendary Redd Foxx and Richard Pryor.

Eddie is married with four children.

Alvin Ailey
(1931–1989)
DANCER AND CHOREOGRAPHER

Ailey spent his early childhood in Rogers, Texas. His family moved to Los Angeles when Ailey was twelve. While on a junior high school class field trip to the Ballet Russe de Monte Carlo, Ailey fell in love with concert dance. He was also inspired by Katherine Dunham's exciting performances at the Lester Horton Dance Theater (the first racially integrated dance company in the country) in 1949. He began his formal training and embarked on a professional career in dance. After Lester Horton's death in 1953, he became director of the company and began to choreograph some of his own pieces. Some of his earliest works included *La Creation du Monde, According to St. Francis, Mourning Morning*, and *Work Dances*.

In 1954, he and his friend, Carmen de Lavallade, were invited to New York City to dance in Truman Capote's Broadway show *House of Flowers*. While in New York, Ailey danced and studied with outstanding artists such as Martha Graham, Doris Humphrey, and Charles Weidman. He took acting classes with Stella Adler. Thereafter, he won several acting roles and continued to choreograph and perform.

In 1958, he founded his own company, the Alvin Ailey American Dance Theater. It made its debut at the 92nd Street YMCA in New York. He served as the company's artistic director from its founding to 1980. The company began its thirteen-week world tour, starting in Australia and the Far East in 1958. Since the first tour, the company has toured extensively in the United States, Europe, and Africa.

Throughout his lifetime, Ailey created seventy-nine ballets, many of which have appeared in the repertoire of major dance companies, including the American Ballet Theatre, the Joffrey Ballet, Dance Theatre of Harlem, Paris Opera Ballet, and La Scala Ballet. He also performed extensively in musical comedies and dramatic shows, in films, and on television. In 1969, he founded the Alvin Ailey American Dance Center, the official school of the Ailey Company, and he went on to form the Repertory Ensemble, the second company, in 1974 and the Ailey Summer Camp.

Throughout his lifetime, Ailey received notable recognition for his achievements and was awarded numerous honorary doctoral degrees. In 1976, he was awarded the Springarm Medal by the NAACP, and in 1982 he received the United Nations Peace Medal. From the world of dance he received a 1975 *Dance Magazine* Award, the Capezio Award (1979), and modern dance's most prestigious prize, the Samuel H. Scripps American Festival Award (1987). In 1988, he was honored by the Kennedy Center for his extraordinary contribution to American culture and achievement in the performing arts. Alvin Ailey died December 1, 1989, but through his highly successful tours on every continent and his unforgettable 79 masterpieces, his visions and legacy will live on.

Savion Glover

(1974–)

DANCER AND CHOREOGRAPHER

Glover was born in Newark, New Jersey, in 1974. An active child from the start, Glover became a "kitchen drummer" at the age of four with pots and pans as his instruments. His passion for percussion passed from his hands to his feet when he enrolled in tap classes three years later at the Broadway Dance Center in New York City. Glover's first seven months of lessons were taken in cowboy boots because his mother couldn't afford tap shoes. After receiving his first real pair of tap shoes, there was no limit to what the young dancer could do.

Growing up in a city like Newark, there were many traps that a young black man like Glover could have fallen into. However, his mother, Yvette, had found a way to channel her son's considerable energies into the performing arts. Yet, she also steered her son clear of the pitfalls of being in the entertainment business. Herself a performer, Yvette was familiar with the not so glamorous side of show business. Glover calls his mother his "main support" and credits her with helping him to have a normal boyhood despite his international success.

When Glover was twelve, he got his first big break when he appeared on Broadway as "The Tap Dance Kid." After performing in the role for a couple of years, Glover went on to do "Black and Blue" in Paris. When the production moved to Broadway, Glover was nominated for a Tony Award. The 1988 film *Tap* bridged the gap between a tap legend and an upstart when Glover danced with the late Sammy Davis, Jr. in one of his last performances. When he portrayed jazz man Jelly Roll Morton in "Jelly's Last Jam" in 1992, Glover proved that the cute kid who had tapped in cowboy boots had grown into a serious artist whose influence was spreading throughout the country. Hines, who co-starred with Glover in the musical, said that the young dancer "redefined the art form" and that he "has steps, speed, clarity, and an invention that no one else ever had."

Savion Glover is considered to be one of the true geniuses of tap. He is credited with blowing the dust off of an art form sometimes stigmatized because of its association with the happy-go-lucky Uncle Tom Negro image. Hailed as "the greatest tap dances that ever lived" by fellow dancer Gregory Hines, Glover continues to tear down misconceptions and promote tap dancing with his passionate, expressive performances.

As a regular character on the popular children's television show Sesame Street, Glover introduced tap to a whole new wide-eyed, eager audience. Glover is excellent in the innovative musical "Bring in 'Da Noise, Bring in 'Da Funk." It provides a moving overview of the challenges African Americans have faced throughout the history of this country through dance, music and poetry. Glover sings, dances, narrates, and provided the choreography for the show.

In 1996, he paid tribute to Gene Kelly at the Academy Awards. He performed in The Wall in 1998. He performed with Stevie Wonder at the 1999 Super Bowl halftime show.

Gregory Hines
(1946–)
ENTERTAINER

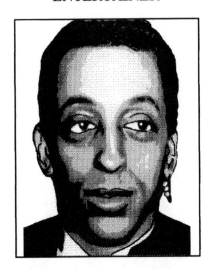

Gregory Hines was born in New York and was blessed with a musically gifted family. Hines was inspired to dance from his father who also danced. Gregory was enrolled in dance school at the age of three. He and his brother Mauriece became professionals before the age of ten as the Hines Kids. They toured America and played in the Apollo Theatre. They studied under the tutelage of Broadway choreographer, Henry LeTang. Hines also was influenced by tap dancers "Sandman" Sims and Teddy Hale.

In 1963, Maurice Hines Sr., joined the act as a percussionist. The trio was billed as Hines, Hines, and Dad. They performed worldwide and were featured on *The Tonight Show* and *The Ed Sullivan Show*.

Hines went solo in 1977 and launched a Broadway career. He received three Tony awards for his stellar performances in *Eubie* (1978), *Comin Uptown* (1979), and *Sophisticated Lady* (1981). The country loved his performances, and he inspired youth and adults to master the craft. One of the men he mentored, Savion Glover, did just that.

Gregory Hines, who is constantly growing, wanted to star in movies. He has starred in more than twenty films, including *Cotton Club, Running Scared, Eve of Destruction, Tap, Rage in Harlem, Preacher's Wife,* and *Waiting to Exhale*.

His current mission is in television. His career has earned him the honor of his own television show with his name. Hines is married with three children.

Miles Davis
(1926–1991)
MUSICIAN

Miles Dewey Davis was born in Alton, Illinois, and grew up in East St. Louis. He collected records and on his 13th birthday was given his first trumpet. By the time he was sixteen, he began playing professionally and received his first real taste of playing jazz when Billy Eckstine's band, which at that time employed Dizzy Gillespie and Charlie Parker, was traveling through and needed to replace a sick horn player. Davis was hired. A fire had been ignited. After high school, in September 1944 Davis enrolled in the Julliard School of Music. He practiced day and night.

In 1945, he did his first recording with the Herbie Fields band and singer "Rubberlegs" Williams. Between 1946 and 1947, he recorded *Now's the Time* and *Koko* in Parker's quintet. Steeped in the bebop tradition and taught by Parker and others, Davis soon became ready to lead with trumpet, horn, and composing.

He transformed jazz into Bebop with his *Birth of the Cool* (1950). As an experiment, in 1950 Davis formed a nine-piece band, with pianist and arranger Gil Evans. They produced *Stella by Starlight* and *Round about Midnight*. Cultivating this cool sound in *Miles Ahead* (1957), Davis and Evans, expanded the idea with the use of a 19-piece orchestra. The band included John Coltrane, Cannonball Adderly, and Herbie Hancock. The Evans-Davis collaboration produced the immensely popular albums *Porgy and Bess* (1958) and *Sketches of Spain* (1960), and *Kind of Blue* (1960).

Davis produced *Nefertiti* in 1967 bridging jazz to rock with fusion. He followed this with *Miles in the Sky* (1968), *Bitches Brew* and *In a Silent Way* in 1969, and *A Tribute to Jack Johnson* in 1970.

Davis retired in 1975 due to health problems. In the 1980s, he returned to do *The Man with the Horn*, *Tutu*, and *Amandla*. He was formerly married to Cicely Tyson. He is survived by two sons.

Dorothy Donegan
(1922–1998)
MUSICIAN

Dorothy was born in Chicago. Donegan began taking piano lessons when she was eight years old. She studied with Rudolph Gantz, the head of the Chicago Musical College. At the age of ten, Dorothy was playing the organ in a church, by the age of fourteen, she was earning money by playing in small clubs on the south side of Chicago. She also studied at the University of Southern California.

Her mother supported her musical studies and served as her first business manager. Her professional concert debut was in 1943 at Orchestra Hall in Chicago. Donegan presented classical music in the first half of her program and jazz in the second. She received rave reviews and her reputation brought her to the attention of Art Tatum who served as her mentor.

In 1944, she appeared in a duet with Eugene Rodgers in the film *Sensations of 1945*. She toured with the Broadway show "Star Time." Dorothy also traveled with Moms Mabley and cut a dozen albums with Continental. During the 1950s and 1960s, she performed in clubs in Los Angeles and New York and commanded $2,000 a week which was top dollar in that era.

Donegan had the ability to adjust with the times. Her career transcended five decades. In 1981, she made a sensational appearance in "Women Blow Their Own Horns" and at the Festival Der Frauen in Hamburg in 1988.

Donegan's performance is described by Whitney Balliet, "On her fast numbers, she swings as hard as any pianist who ever lived, and on slow ballads, she is delicate as a rose."

Donegan's albums include *Explosive Dorothy Donegan; Live at the 1990 Floating Jazz Festival; The Incredible Dorothy Donegan; I Just Want to Sing; Piano Retrospective;* and *Dorothy Romps.*

She had one son.

Wynton Marsalis
(1961–)
MUSICIAN

Wynton Marsalis' performances and recordings have encouraged both the popularity of jazz music and its acceptance as a serious art form. Born in New Orleans and reared in nearby Kenner, Louisiana, Marsalis was surrounded by New Orleans jazz. His father, Ellis Marsalis, was a gifted professional jazz musician and teacher and had a profound influence on the development of Wynton's respect for the jazz tradition. Marsalis' brothers, Branford and Delfayo, became professional musicians as well.

Beginning with trumpet lessons at age twelve, Marsalis went on to attend the Berkshire Music Center at Tanglewood in Massachusetts and the Julliard School of Music in New York City. At age twenty, he toured with Art Blakey's Jazz Messengers and jazz pianist and composer Herbie Hancock's V.S.O.P. quartet. In 1981, he released *Wynton Marsalis*, his debut album as a jazz bandleader, and in 1983 he released *Trumpet Concertos*, his classical music recording debut. He decided to focus on jazz in the mid-1980s and has continued to go on tours and make records. In 1984 became the first musician to Grammy Awards in both jazz and classical categories in the same year.

Early in his career, Marsalis was regarded as a master technician of the trumpet. He reached new heights of creative expression with his recordings *Majesty of the Blues* (1989) and the subsequent trilogy *Soul Gestures in Southern Blue* (1991). These works represent a return to his New Orleans jazz and blues roots, although the music is distinctively contemporary. In 1993, he released *Citi Movement*, a score for a modern ballet and perhaps his most ambitious project up to that time. Like jazz composer Duke Ellington, Marsalis' compositions combined elements of classical music with original jazz improvisation. Also in 1993, he resumed his classical music career, performing with opera soprano Kathleen Battle. Wynton is a tireless musician and continues to produce great music including *In this House-On this Morning, Joe Cool's Blues, Blood on Fields, Midnight Blues,* and *Marsalis on Music* which is also a book. His other book is *Sweet Song Blues on the Road.* Wynton did the soundtrack for *Rosewood.*

Marsalis has influenced a generation of young musicians and listeners and is credited with promoting the resurgence of traditional jazz music and its popular following. Since 1990, he has been the artistic director for the Jazz at Lincoln Center program in New York City. Wynton has received numerous honorary doctorates.

Thomas Dorsey
(1899–1993)
MUSICIAN

Thomas Dorsey was born in Villa Rica, Georgia. He played the piano during the revival services while his father, a traveling Baptist minister, preached. To help support his family, he began playing in saloons at the tender age of eleven. His stage name was "Georgia Tom." Dorsey moved to Chicago at the age of seventeen to study music at the Chicago College of Composition and Arrangement.

In the 1920s, Georgia Tom performed with several jazz and blues bands. His own band, the Wildcats Jazz Band released "Riverside Blues," "Tight Like That," and "Terrible Operations Blues."

Dorsey never forgot his religious upbringing. His song, "Somebody Somewhere," was included in the National Baptist Convention's *Gospel Pearls Collection.* In the late 1920s he decided to devote his talents exclusively to gospel music. He formed the world's finest gospel choir at Ebenezer Church in Chicago. He started a publishing company devoted exclusively to the sale of gospel and sheet music. He became the lifelong choir director at Pilgrim Baptist Church. He founded the National Convention of Gospel Choirs and Choruses to train gospel vocal groups and soloists.

In 1931, tragedy beset Dorsey. He lost his wife and daughter in childbirth. The Lord used him to write "Take My Hand, Precious Lord," which became his trademark song. He went on to write more than 1,000 songs praising the name of his Savior Jesus. He presided over the convention for forty years, promoting gospel music worldwide.

John Coltrane
(1926–1967)
MUSICIAN

John Coltrane was born in Hamlet, North Carolina. He loved music as a child, and many family members and friends predicted a musical career. In high school, he played with various bands. In 1944, Coltrane moved to Philadelphia and studied at the Ornstein School of Music. During World War II, he played with the U.S. Navy Band. Coltrane was very gifted and could play soprano, alto, and tenor saxophone, and flute equally well.

Coltrane was blessed to learn and play with some of the best African American musicians in the country, including Miles Davis, McCoy Tyner, Pharaoh Sanders, and Thelonious Monk. In 1955, Coltrane took a special liking to Miles Davis and played with his band. They had similar views on music and were not afraid to be viewed as different and eccentric. Davis and Coltrane were willing to take risks with their music.

In 1960, he formed his own quartet. He would practice for long hours. He produced 37 albums including *A Love of Supreme; Blue Train; Soultrane; Interstellar Space; Kulu Se Mama; Selflessness; Expression; Giant Steps; My Favorite Things; The Complete African Brass; Crescent, Meditations;* and *The Complete Works of John Coltrane.* He is considered by many critics, the most influential jazz musician in the twentieth century. In 1984, the John Coltrane Cultural Society was founded in Philadelphia, to preserve his legacy and teach children to love music.

Coltrane is survived by his wife Alice and three children. She played piano in his band and produced several of his albums posthumously.

Aretha Franklin
(1942–)
SINGER

Aretha Franklin, the Queen of Soul, was born in Memphis, Tennessee. She, her two sisters and one brother were abandoned by their mother. Her father C.L. Franklin, a prominent minister in Detroit, and her aunt Clara Ward gave the children a strong spiritual and musical foundation. The legendary James Cleveland worked with Franklin on gospel music when she was nine. Family friends Mahalia Jackson and Sam Cooke encouraged her recording career.

Her voice covers five octaves, and the state of Michigan declared it a natural resource. At 14, she belted out "Precious Lord" in front of 4,500 parishioners. Columbia Records producer John Hammond signed her that same year and compared her to the great Billie Holiday. Later, she moved from their pop/jazz orchestrations to R&B style. Under the direction of Jerry Wexler, during the late '60s, she made several hits, including "Respect." In 1968, she was the first African American woman to make the cover of *Time Magazine*. In the 1980s, she moved to Arista records, and her album, "Who's Zoomin Who," went platinum.

Aretha has had to overcome many obstacles in her life. There have been several divorces, parenting challenges, tax problems, alcoholism, a pathological fear of flying brought on by a near plane accident, and her father being killed by a burglar. She has become very resilient over her almost fifty-year career.

The Queen of Soul has won fifteen Grammies, recorded twenty number 1 R&B hits, and was the first female inducted into the Rock & Roll Hall of Fame in 1987. She has performed at the presidential inaugurations of Jimmy Carter and Bill Clinton. She continues to change with the times by working with Luther Vandross, Kenneth "Baby Face" Edmonds, Lauryn Hill, and Sean "Puffy" Combs.

Aretha has four children.

Stevie Wonder
(1950–)
SINGER

Stevland Judkins Morris was born in 1950 in Saginaw, Michigan. Although no one can be sure of what led to the premature infant's blindness, it is believed that he was supplied with too much oxygen while he was in his incubator. Whether he was born without sight or his condition was caused by carelessness, Wonder has lived his entire life in visual darkness. However, he never allowed his blindness to be a disability. Because he was one of six children, Stevie's siblings did not fully understand that blindness was often viewed as a limitation to performing common activities. Therefore, Stevie was expected to do many of the things that sighted children could do—and he did them. This environment taught Stevie that not only was he not inferior to other children, but, as he would later recall, he "believed that God had something for me to do."

By the time he was eleven years old, he was singing and playing the piano, harmonica, and drums. He was such a skillful entertainer that he was brought to the attention of Motown Records president Berry Gordy. Gordy recognized Stevie's considerable potential and made him a part of the Motown family.

In 1963, thirteen-year-old Stevie's performance of "Fingertips, Part 2" rose to the top of the U.S. pop charts. The next few years saw the release of such R&B classics as "Uptight," "I Was Made to Love Her," and "For Once in My Life." By the time he was only eighteen years old, Wonder had produced enough hit singles for his first *Greatest Hits* compilation.

Songs like Wonder's "Superstition," "Sir Duke," and "You Are the Sunshine of My Life" were so well received by music critics and audiences alike that even the most talented recording artists had trouble competing with Wonder. Marvin Gaye, one of soul music's greatest vocalists and songwriters, once said, "What artist in his right mind wouldn't be intimidated by Stevie Wonder?" As Wonder's music developed deeper meaning, his songs began to reflect his active support for various causes, including a campaign against South Africa's apartheid system, a crackdown on drunk driving, and the enactment of a national holiday in honor of Dr. Martin Luther King.

In 1989, he was inducted in the Rock & Roll Hall of Fame. In 1991, he produced the soundtrack for Spike Lee's film *Jungle Fever.* In 1992, he signed a multimillion dollar lifetime contract with Motown Records. Wonder's halftime performance at the 1999 Super Bowl with tap dancer Savion Glover was considered awesome.

Wonder owns KJLH (Joy, Love, Happiness) in Los Angeles. He has four children.

Whitney Houston
(1963–)
SINGER

Whitney Houston was born in East Orange, New Jersey, to a musical family. Her mother, Cissy, sang gospel and did backup work for Aretha Franklin and Elvis Presley. Her cousins are Dionne and Dee Dee Warwick. Her father manages her company, her brother Michael is her road manager, and her brother Gary is a backup singer. Whitney married award-winning singer Bobby Brown.

At the age of nine, Whitney began singing at New Hope Baptist Church. She sang with her mother at various concerts. She modeled throughout high school while maintaining honor roll status. In 1985, she released her first album, *Whitney Houston,* which included "How Will I Know?" "Greatest Love of All," "All at Once," and "You Give Good Love." It won a Grammy and two national music awards and sold thirteen million copies.

In 1987, she released *Whitney,* which included, "Where Do Broken Hearts Go?" She won another Grammy, two Emmys, and ten American Music awards. This album sold more than the previous one. Her third album, *I'm Your Baby Tonight* (1990), went double platinum and also won many awards.

Her fourth album debuted her acting career in *The Bodyguard.* She won every award imaginable, and it sold thirty-three million copies, more than any other sound track in history. She also played stellar roles in *Waiting to Exhale, Preacher's Wife,* and *Cinderella.* Houston is the executive producer of her own studio, which produced *Cinderella,* and has acquired the rights to produce *The Dorothy Dandridge Story.*

Houston has sold more than 100 million copies. She established the Whitney Houston Foundation for Children to combat illiteracy. She is a major contributor to the United Negro College Fund, AIDS research, and organizations in Newark. She has received thousands of awards, including the Sammy Davis, Jr., Award for top entertainer of the year in 1994. Her latest release is *My Love is Your Love.*

She and her husband Bobby have one daughter.

Nat King Cole
(1919–1965)
SINGER

Nat King Cole was born in Montgomery, Alabama, and was blessed with a musical family. His mother was a choir director. His father was a pastor and his three brothers were musicians.

Cole learned music in high school and played piano in his father's church. He organized his first jazz group, the Musical Dukes, and they were well received in the community. He moved to Los Angeles and performed in nightclubs. He formed the King Cole Trio with Oscar Moore (guitar) and Wesley Prince (bass), and they received great fame. The song "Straighten Up and Fly Right" increased their success.

The public began to realize that although Cole was a good pianist, his voice was silky and unique. They wanted him to play less and sing more, Cole complied.

In 1948, he hosted his own radio show. In 1956, he hosted his own television show. He continued to travel the country, singing to sold-out audiences. Hollywood saw gold in this brilliant singer. Cole appeared in *Breakfast in Hollywood, China Gate, St. Louis Blues,* and *Cat Ballou,* among others.

Cole was influenced by the work of Earl Hines and Billy Eckstine. He received many awards. He is part of the Hollywood Walk of Fame. Nat King Cole died much too soon of cancer. The public continues to remember his melodic voice.

Nat is survived by a wife and two daughters. Cole passed the musical tradition to his daughters, Natalie and Carol.

Mahalia Jackson
(1911–1972)
SINGER

Mahalia Jackson was born in New Orleans, Louisiana into a family of poverty. She had five siblings. She began singing at the age of four at Plymouth Rock Church. She decided at an early age that she was not going to compromise and sing blues, jazz, or R&B. She would only sing gospel for her Lord.

Jackson moved to Chicago in 1927 and met Tommy Dorsey. He became her mentor and brother in Christ. Her first album was *God Shall Wipe Away All Your Tears*. Her second, *Move on Up a Little Higher*, sold eight million copies to Black fans. Record companies took notice. They wanted Jackson to cross over and sing other genres, but she remained true to her childhood promise and would not be bought with the promise of more money. Besides, gospel artists did not have to rely on anyone outside their race to succeed. She went on to record thirty albums, twelve of which went gold. Her greatest hits included "Just Over the Hill," "He's Got the Whole World in His Hand," and "How I Got Over."

Jackson had the honor of singing at the inauguration ceremonies of Truman, Eisenhower, Kennedy, and Johnson. Her greatest honor came in 1963, when she sang before Martin Luther King, Jr., spoke at the March on Washington. She sang, "I been Buked and I been Scorned," and she sang her heart out.

Jackson was considered the world's greatest gospel singer. A biographical movie was made about her titled *The Power and the Glory*. She had her own CBS radio and television program and managed several businesses and real estate properties.

James Brown
(1928–)

SINGER

James Brown was born in Macon, Georgia. His rise from juvenile delinquent to Soul Brother number 1 is one of the great modern-day American success stories. The only child of a poor backwoods family, he was sent to Augusta, Georgia, when he was five years old to live in his aunt's brothel. He earned his keep by running errands for soldiers at nearby Camp Gordon, entertaining them with his buckdancing, and enticing them into his aunt's establishment. Beginning as a gospel singer in the late 1940s, Brown learned to play the drums, organ, and piano. Singing gospel music and playing piano, drums, and guitar served as an emotional outlet for the young Brown.

In 1952 he settled in Georgia and joined the Gospel Starlighters, a quartet led by Bobby Byrd. Eventually, the Starlighters evolved into a rhythm and blues outfit and changed their name to the Avons, later the Flames. In November 1955, while based in Macon, Georgia the Famous Flames cut a demo at radio station WIBB of their tune *Please, Please, Please.* Record producer Ralph Bass heard the demo, and was so impressed by Brown's impassioned lead and the group's hard harmonies that he immediately signed them to King Records. Two months later, the song hit number 5 on Billboard's R&B chart. Brown has made 98 songs to reach Billboard's top 40, a record unsurpassed by any other artist.

Although Brown was virtually ignored by the American mass market throughout much of his career, he recorded more than forty gold records. *Please, Please, Please* (1956) was a success in England and was his first top-selling single in the United States. *Try Me* (1958) also became a gold record.

Brown dominated the rhythm-and-blues market with *Prisoner of Love* (1963), *I Got You* (1965), *Papa's Got a Brand New Bag* (1965), and *It's a Man's World* (1966). *Cold Sweat* was a top single in 1967, followed by *Say It Loud, I'm Black and I'm Proud* (1968). His innovations during this period had a profound influence on popular music styles around the world, including funk, rock, afro-pop, disco, and eventually hip-hop. Rappers love using his music on their songs.

He wrote his autobiography, *James Brown, The Godfather of Soul,* in 1986, and that same year, was one of the first inductees into the Rock 'N' Roll Hall of Fame. In 1988, Brown was sentenced to six years in prison for assault and for eluding police during a car chase. He was paroled in 1991 and resumed his music career, recording *Love Over-Due* that same year. In 1992, he received a Grammy Lifetime Achievement Award. He continues to produce in the studio with *When We Were Kings.* In 1995, he was inducted into the Music Hall of Fame.

Reverend Al Sharpton's hairstyle is in honor of James Brown. Brown is a widow with four children.

Janet Jackson
(1966–)
SINGER

Janet Jackson was born in Gary, Indiana, the youngest of nine children. She was born into a musical family. Her father had a group called the Falcons. Her brothers were just becoming discovered at the time of her birth. She performed with the Jackson 5 at the age of seven. Janet was always viewed as the baby, a tomboy, and chubby. Few people expected what would ultimately happen in her career.

Janet took a different route from her brothers. She chose acting over singing and co-starred in *Good Times, Different Strokes,* and *Fame.* In 1982, at the age of sixteen, she released her album *Janet,* which was moderately successful. In 1986, she decided to utilize the services of producers Jimmy Jam and Terry Lewis on her next album, *Control.* The partnership worked. The album sold more than four million copies, and Virgin Records signed her to an $80 million contract. The trio was not done yet. In 1989, they released *Rhythm Nation 1814,* which sold six million.

Janet Jackson, who performs with the same intensity and creativity as her brother Michael Jackson, sings and dances before sold-out audiences around the world. Fans loved when Michael and Janet got together for a Motown television special. Janet extended her acting career in *Poetic Justice* with the late Tupac.

Her latest releases are *Design of a Decade, Velvet Rope,* and *Go Deep.* All have gone platinum. She has sold more than 40 million records worldwide.

Michael Jackson
(1958–)
SINGER

Michael Jackson was born in Gary, Indiana, the seventh of nine children. His father had a group called the Falcons. Five of the boys began singing around the house and performed in talent shows at school. They became the Gary city champs and repeated their success in Chicago.

Their first hit was in 1967 with "Big Boy." This record led to appearances at the Apollo Theater, the David Frost Show, and the Ed Sullivan Show. Gladys Knight actually discovered them for Motown in 1966, Diana Ross was extremely supportive, and Suzanne de Passe trained them.

All this took place before Jackson's tenth birthday. Because he was the lead singer on 90% of the songs, the crowd raved over him. Unfortunately, Michael lost his childhood. He never did simple things like playing ball or walk the dog. His father managed the Jackson brothers, and practice became a full-time job. Early hits included "I Want You Back" and "I'll Be There," which they performed on an ABC television special. In 1971, Michael went solo with the big hit "Got to Be There."

In 1979, he left Motown because he wanted greater control of his music. Michael also removed his father from his management duties. He teamed with Quincy Jones and produced *Off the Wall*, which sold eight million copies. In 1982, they did *Thriller* and more than 46 million copies sold. All of his albums are dedicated to his mother.

Michael is a consummate performer. His Moonwalk dance took the country by storm, along with the *Billie Jean* and *Thriller* videos. He reunited with his brothers for the Victory Tour, and they provided spellbinding performances.

Jackson performed for Hollywood in *The Wiz*. He showed his business savvy with the acquisition of most of the Beatles' music. He helped spearhead the production of *We Are the World* and proceeds were contributed to help children in underdeveloped countries in 1991.

Other albums include *Bad*, *Dangerous*, and *History*. All have gone platinum. Michael is married and they have two children.

Queen Latifah
(1970–)

SINGER

Queen Latifah was born Dana Owens in Newark, New Jersey, the second of two children. Her mother, Rita, is a major influence on Latifah and is involved in the management of the company. A Muslim cousin gave her the name Latifah, which means delicate and sensitive in Arabic, when she was eight. Latifah added Queen when she became a performer.

Queen Latifah sang in many plays in school. She used her height (5'10") to become a power forward on the high school basketball team. She was the only senior to win four awards: Most Popular, Best All Around, Most Comical, and Best Dancer. While in high school, she formed a rap group, Ladies Fresh. Later they became Flavor Unit.

In 1988, Queen released her first single, *Wrath of My Madness and Princess of the Posse*, which was followed by *Dance for Me*. She performed at the Apollo, and toured Europe. In 1989, she released her first album, *All Hail the Queen*, which sold more than a million copies. This was followed with *Black Reign, Nature of a Sista, Unity*, and *Order in the Court*. She won a Grammy for *Unity*, and each album outperformed the last.

Early on Queen realized the need to understand the business. She created Flavor Unit Management Company. Flavor has signed more than 20 rap groups, including Naughty by Nature. She partnered with Motown for distribution. She also owns a video store, a delicatessen, and other businesses.

Latifah is also an actress. Her movies include *House Party II, Juice, Jungle Fever*, and *Set It Off*. She was the star in the award-winning television series *Living Single*, where she played Khadijah. Future movies include *Living Out Loud* and *Bessie Smith*, among others.

In 1999, she released her biography: *Ladies First: Revelations from a Strong Woman.*

William "Smokey" Robinson
(1940–)
SINGER

He was born in Detroit and could be found singing in the bathroom or on the corner. His uncle named him "Smokey" to always remind him of his "blackness." His house was full of music and Sarah Vaughn was Smokey's foundation.

The name of the original group was the Matadors. They met Berry Gordy because of a lead they got from Jackie Wilson's staff. Berry was impressed with the group, but more with Smokey's writing skills and voice. The group changed its name to the Miracles in 1957. Their first big hit *Shop Around* in 1960 sold more than a million copies. The Miracles went on to produce many gold albums with songs such as *Ooo Baby Baby, Tracks of My Tears, Going to a Go Go, Tears of a Clown, More Love, Baby Baby Don't Cry,* and *I Second That Emotion.*

Berry and Smokey grew closer. Smokey wrote hits for many Motown groups, including *My Girl* for the Temptations, *Ain't that Peculiar* for Marvin Gaye, *My Guy* for Mary Wells, *The Hunter Gets Captured by the Game* for the Marvelettes, and *Still Water* for the Four Tops. When Motown released their Top 40, Smokey was involved in 27 songs.

In 1972, Smokey went solo and continued to write and sing hits. Songs included *Quiet Storm, Crusin, Being with You,* and *Just to See Her.* The latter won a Grammy, they all went gold, and many radio stations called their love format "Quiet Storm."

Gordy promoted Robinson to vice-president. Smokey's career has now moved into the fourth decade and he remains a major draw on the concert circuit. Smokey has three children.

Thelma "Butterfly" McQueen
(1911–)
ACTRESS

Thelma McQueen was born in Tampa, Florida. Her parents divorced when she was five years old, and her mother moved to New York. After high school, McQueen became a dancer in Venezuela Jones's Negro Youth Group. She studied dance under the great Katherine Dunham. In 1935, she made her stage debut as part of the Butterfly Ballet. Her nickname remained with her thereafter.

McQueen made her Broadway debut in 1937 in the production *Brown Sugar*. Her favorable review caught the attention of many directors. Her voice was higher than soprano and she was funny. Her claim to fame was landing the role of Prissy in *Gone with the Wind*. It was a major production that required two years of filming. She said that one day's income paid for a semester at UCLA, where she was enrolled.

McQueen played Prissy extremely well, but she was in constant disagreement with the director. She resented stereotypes. For example, she refused to eat watermelon. She objected to Rhett Butler calling her a derogatory name. She complained about the head attire for Black actors. The major issue was when Miss Scarlett slapped Prissy. She objected and the compromise was that a sound would be made when it appeared that she was being slapped.

McQueen was in constant disagreement with Hattie McDaniel, who believed that playing a maid was better than being one. Although she received great reviews for playing Prissy, there were very few roles for Black actors outside of mammies, which Butterfly refused playing. Her integrity cost her dearly, but what good is it to gain the whole world and lose your soul?

She enjoyed playing in *Cabin in the Sky* in 1943. The all-star cast included Duke Ellington, Louis Armstrong, Ethel Waters, Ruby Dandridge, and others. Her other film credits included *The Women, Affectionately Yours, I Dood It, Mildred Pierce, Flame of Barbary Coast, Duel in the Sun, Killer Diller, The Phynx, Amazing Grace, Mosquito Coast, Polly,* and *Stiff.* Her television productions were *The Beulah Show, Green Pastures, Seven Wishes of Joanna Peabody,* and *Our World.*

At age sixty-four, she completed her bachelor's degree from New York City College. She said, "Show business is only my hobby; community service is my work."

Ossie Davis
(1917–)
ACTOR

Ruby Dee
(1924–)
ACTRESS

Ossie was born in Cogdell, Georgia, the oldest of five children. He grew up in a home full of preachers and storytellers. Ossie won scholarships to Tuskegee and Howard. His aunts generated the funds to send him to Howard. He earned a bachelor's degree in 1939.

Ruby was born in Cleveland and was raised with her siblings in New York. She studied music and literature under the watchful eye of her mother. Ruby received her B.A. in English from Hunter College.

Ossie and Ruby met while performing in the Broadway play *Jeb* in 1945. They were married in 1948. Ossie said in *Newsday*, "Ruby was my colleague, then she became my friend and eventually my wife." They performed together on stage in *Anna Lucasta, A Raisin in the Sun*, and *Purlie Victorious.* They had a radio show called the *Ossie Davis and Ruby Dee Story Hour* and a television show *Ossie and Ruby.* On the silver screen, they played in Spike Lee's *Do the Right Thing* and *Jungle Fever.*

Ossie also appeared in *Gone Are the Days* and *Get on the Bus;* on television, he appeared in *The Emperor Jones, Teacher Teacher, Defenders, The Fugitive, The Secret Path*, and *Bonanza.* He directed *Cotton Comes to Harlem, Kongi's Harvest*, and *Gordon's War.*

Ruby's film credits include *Love in Syncopation, The Jackie Robinson Story, Go Man Go, Take a Giant Step, Virgin Island, The Incident*, and *Black Girl.* Her television appearances include *Wedding Band, Roots: The Next Generation, The Fugitive, Having Our Say, Peyton Place*, and *I Know Why the Caged Bird Sings.* She received an Emmy nomination for *East Side, West Side* and won for her role in for *Decoration Day.*

Davis and Dee are frequent guests on PBS shows, and they often narrate fairy tales for children on audio cassette. Ruby has also written *Two Ways to Count to Ten* and *Tower to Heaven* for children and *My One Good Nerve* for adults.

Ossie and Ruby have been very active in the civil rights movement and have organized actors to take political positions. Ossie spoke at Malcolm X's funeral. They have created numerous scholarships and opportunities for young people to perfect their craft in the arts.

Their marriage has produced three children. Their autobiography, *In This Life Together*, chronicles their career and their 50-year-old marriage.

155

Dorothy Dandridge
(1922–1965)

ACTRESS

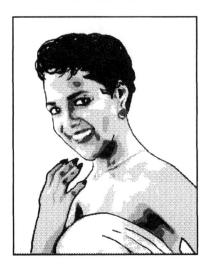

Dorothy Dandridge was born in Cleveland. She was often viewed as a woman before her time. Widely recognized for her classically stunning beauty and her talents as an actress and singer, Dandridge confounded Hollywood, which portrayed Black women only as mammies and servants. The film industry was not ready to accept a Black actress with beauty, grace, and style.

Dandridge broke several barriers for Black actresses in Hollywood. She was among the first to play a leading lady role in a major motion picture. She also holds the dubious distinction of being the first Black woman to be embraced by a White man on the silver screen (*Island in the Sun*, 1957).

Dorothy and her older sister Vivian sang in Black churches across the country. In 1936, the Dandridge Sisters performed at the famous Cotton Club in New York City. The success of the act landed them a regular spot in the lineup. The following year, the Dandridge Sisters appeared in their first film, *A Day at the Races*. The act soon broke up, and as a performer, Dandridge was on her own.

The 1940s were challenging times for Dandridge. In 1942, she married Harold Nicholas, one half of the dance team The Nicholas Brothers, who had also been regular performers at the Cotton Club. A year later, she gave birth to her daughter, Harolyn. When Harolyn was diagnosed as severely retarded, Dandridge vowed that she would do all that she could to care for the child herself. Despite her love and devotion to her daughter, Dandridge was not able to provide the kind of attention Harolyn needed. Harolyn had to be institutionalized. During the same time, Dandridge's troubled marriage to Nicholas ended. Alone again, Dandridge traveled the world as a nightclub singer.

As for her career, the 1950s proved to be more prosperous. In 1951, she became the first Black entertainer to grace the stage of the Empire Room in New York's Waldorf-Astoria Hotel. In 1954, Dandridge landed the role which made her famous in the all-Black musical *Carmen Jones*, with Harry Belafonte and Diahann Carroll. The film was a success, and it earned Dandridge an Oscar nomination for best actress. No other Black actress had ever received that level of critical recognition. Other films include *Sundown, Lady from Louisiana, Bahama Passage, Drums of the Congo, Atlantic City, Pillow to Post, Tarzan's Peril, The Harlem Globetrotters, Bright Road, Porgy and Bess*, and *Malaga*.

After *Island in the Sun*, *The Decks Ran Red* (1958), and *Tamango* (1960), nonstereotypical roles once again became scarce for Dandridge. She returned to singing in nightclubs. After another short-lived marriage and several risky investments gone bad, Dandridge found herself bankrupt and unable to find work. Sometimes referred to as "the Black Marilyn Monroe," Dandridge was found dead in her apartment from an overdose of antidepressants on September 8, 1965. She is survived by two children.

Since the mid-1990s, there has been a growing interest in the life and tragic death of Dandridge. Several studios have been vying for the rights to put the events of Dandridge's life on the silver screen. Whitney Houston has bought the rights for the film and has chosen Halle Berry to play Dandridge.

Morgan Freeman
(1937–)
ACTOR

Morgan Freeman was born in Memphis, Tennessee. While still an infant, he was sent to live with his maternal grandmother in Charleston, Mississippi. She died when Freeman was six years old. He spent his childhood with relatives in Chicago, Nashville and Mississippi. He entered the Air Force in 1955.

He attended acting school in Los Angeles in 1959. His acting debut was on Broadway in the play *Hello Dolly* in 1968. He won a Tony nomination for the *Mighty Gents* in 1978. Freeman performed in *Coriolanus* in 1979 for the New York Shakespeare Festival. He won Obies awards for this, and *The Gospel at Colonus*. He performed *A Soldier's Play* with the Negro Ensemble in 1981. This brilliant actor did not receive a leading role until he was fifty years old.

After Broadway, he worked with PBS and Electric Company in the show *Easy Reader*. In 1987, he was nominated for best supporting actor in *Street Smart*. In 1989, he was nominated for best actor in *Driving Miss Daisy*. He repeated this feat in 1995 with *Shawshank Redemption*. He has performed in many movies, including *Glory, Unforgiven, Lean on Me, Kiss the Girls, Deep Impact, The Flood, The Big Hit,* and *Amistad.* He is one of the few actors whose parts transcend race. Morgan commented in *Essence*, "I've been offered Black quasi-heroes who get hanged at the end. I won't do a part like that. He has to live throughout the movie."

His directing debut was in the film *Bopha* about apartheid. Freeman lives on a 120-acre farm in Mississippi. He is married with four children.

Angela Bassett
(1958–)
ACTRESS

Angela Bassett was born in New York and raised in St. Petersburg, Florida. She grew up in a housing project with her mother and sister and became interested in acting at a young age. In 1974, she had witnessed critically acclaimed actor James Earl Jones' powerful role in *Of Mice and Men*. It moved Bassett to tears.

Bassett applied to Yale University. Always an excellent student, Bassett was accepted and spent six years at the prestigious institution, earning a bachelor's degree and a master's degree. Bassett's southern background led to slight problems in adjusting to the East Coast setting of the school.

Soon after graduating from Yale in 1982, Bassett began acting in commercials. She landed a brief role on the television soap opera *The Guiding Light* and minor parts in several movies, like *Critters 4*. She starred in August Wilson's *Ma Rainey's Black Bottom* (on Broadway) and *Joe Turner's Come and Gone*. She also appeared in John Sayles's 1991 movie *City of Hope*. In John Singleton's *Boyz n the Hood*, Bassett played the mother of the lead character, Tre.

The year 1992 was a busy one for the up-and-coming actress. Bassett appeared in John Sayles's *Passion Fish*. She also played Katherine Jackson, mother of Michael and Janet, in the TV miniseries *The Jacksons: An American Dream*, produced by Suzanne de Passe. However, her most memorable work in 1992 by far was as Betty Shabazz, wife of the slain civil rights leader in Spike Lee's *Malcolm X*. *Premiere* magazine called her performance "the best work she's ever done on film."

Bassett's talents as an actress were nearly universally proclaimed when she portrayed the life of the legendary rock 'n' roll diva Tina Turner in the film *What's Love Got to Do with It*. Because he was so confident of her abilities as an actress, longtime friend and costar, Laurence Fishburne, would not accept the role of Ike Turner until he was assured that Bassett would play Tina. Fishburne stated, "Angela becomes who she's playing. It's like she's not there anymore. Angela can do anything." She was nominated for an Oscar.

Bassett has also appeared in popular favorites such as Terry McMillan's *Waiting to Exhale* with Whitney Houston and *How Stella Got Her Groove Back* with Whoopi Goldberg. Her film credits include *Storm, Heroes of Desert, Innocent Blood, Vampire in Brooklyn, Strange Days, Contact, Africa in America, Revolution*, and *Judgment Day*. Angela just recently married.

Denzel Washington
(1954–)
ACTOR

Denzel Washington was born in Mt. Vernon, New York, the son of a Pentecostal minister. He won a scholarship to an upper New York state, predominantly White boarding school. He was a premed student at Fordham University. During a YMCA–sponsored summer camp, he organized a talent show for the youth, but the audience recognized his natural talent. Washington returned to Fordham in the fall, auditioned for the university's production of *The Emperor Jones,* and won the part over theater majors. He went on to play *Othello* and was compared to Paul Robeson. New York agents took notice.

After graduation in 1981, Denzel Washington performed in the television drama *Wilma,* which was based on the life of Wilma Rudolph. He acted with George Segal in *Carbon Copy.* An important catalyst to his career was his role as a doctor in *St. Else*where, which he played for five years (1982-1987). He won an Obie Award for his stage performance in *Soldier's Story* and also starred in the film version. In 1989, he was nominated for an Oscar for his role as Steve Biko in *Cry Freedom.*

He was a bona fide star. This was only the fourth time an African American actor had been nominated or had won. Hollywood knew they had a star but did not know how to use him outside of predominantly Black films. In 1990, Denzel Washington won an Academy Award for best supporting actor in *Glory.* Many African Americans felt he should have won again in his portrayal of *Malcolm X,* directed by Spike Lee.

Washington's film résumé also includes *Hank Aaron, The Preacher's Wife, Devil in a Blue Dress, Much Ado about Nothing, Bone Collector, Mo' Better Blues, Philadelphia, Pelican Brief, Crimson Tide, Fallen, Siege,* and *He Got Game.* Hollywood now understands that Denzel Washington is a major attraction to all audiences. He is one of the few actors who can command $12–15 million per film.

Denzel Washington has received numerous awards, but his priorities are clear. In an interview with the *Washington Post,* he said, "Acting is just a way of living. Family is life." He and his wife have four children and contribute to many charitable causes.

Cicely Tyson
(1933–)
ACTRESS

Cicely Tyson was born in New York and began her career as a model. She studied at New York University and the Actors Studio. She then acted on Broadway. In 1959, Tyson decided to pursue film roles in Hollywood. Her major concern was Hollywood's stereotypical images of Black women who were projected as either mammies or sluts. Tyson would not compromise her principles by accepting such demeaning parts. She was also concerned about the longevity of a Hollywood career. Unlike White men, who could perform until death, she noticed that once Black women's beauty began to fade, so did their careers.

She decided it was worth a try, but under her terms. She would play only roles that brought dignity to African American women. She accepted the reality that there would be many days of unemployment. Fortunately, Hollywood recognized Tyson's talents. Her list of films is incredible and includes *Sounder* (nominated for an Oscar), *Roots, Autobiography of Miss Jane Pittman, Women of Brewster Place, A Woman Called Moses, A Hero Ain't Nothin but a Sandwich, Always Outnumbered, Mama Flora's Family, Heat Wave, The Kid Who Loved Christmas, King, The Heart Is a Lonely Hunter, Fried Green Tomatoes, Hoodlum, Price of Heaven, Ms. Scrooge, The Road to Galveston, Riot, Duplicates, Samaritan, The Mitch Snyder Story, Acceptable Risks, Intimate Encounters, Playing with Fire, Benny's Place, Just an Old Sweet Son, River Niger, Blue Bird, The Comedians, A Man Called Adam,* and *The Last Angry Man,* among others. She won an Emmy in 1994 for the television miniseries, *Oldest Living Confederate Widow Tells All.*

Tyson practices the scripture "To whom much is given, much is required." She is one of the founding members of the Dance Theatre of Harlem in 1976. She created the Cicely Tyson School of Performing Arts in East Orange, New Jersey.

She was formerly married to Miles Davis.

Whoopi Goldberg
(1955–)
ACTRESS

Born Caryn Jones in New York City, Whoopi Goldberg began performing at the age of eight at the Helena Rubinstein Children's Theatre and Children's Program at the Hudson Guild from 1958 to 1960. In 1975, she moved to California and became a founding member of the San Diego Repertory Theatre, where she played the title roles in Bertolt Brecht's *Mother Courage* and Marsha Norman's *Getting Out.* As a member of an improvisational group called Spontaneous Combustion, an improvisational group, she honed her comedic skills.

Later, Goldberg moved to the Bay Area and joined the Blake Street Hawkeyes Theatre in Berkeley. Moving quickly into solo performances, Goldberg created *The Spook Show* (1983–1984), which first played in San Francisco and then toured the United States and Europe. It was at a 1983 performance of that show, performed at the Dance Theatre Workshop in New York City, that Whoopi caught the attention of director Mike Nichols. He offered to present her in an evening of her own original material on Broadway. The show opened at the Lyceum Theater to critical acclaim. She later taped the show as an HBO special, "Whoopi Goldberg Direct from Broadway." The record album of her Broadway show came to the attention of Steven Spielberg, who was casting his film version of Alice Walker's novel *The Color Purple.*

The Color Purple launched Goldberg's film career. In addition to an Oscar nomination for her role as Celie, she won the 1985 Golden Globe Award for Best Performance by an Actress in a Dramatic Motion Picture and the NAACP's Image Award for Best Actress in a Motion Picture. She has hosted the Oscars on several occasions.

Since *The Color Purple,* she has starred in such motion pictures as *Jumpin' Jack Flash, Burglar, Fatal Beauty* (for which she earned a second Image Award), *Clara's Heart, Ghost, The Long Walk Home* (earning her a third Image Award), *Soapdish,* and Robert Altman's *The Player.* Her performance as Oda Mae Brown in *Ghost*—the highest-grossing movie of 1990—earned her the Academy Award for Best Supporting Actress. Her film credits also include her Image Award-nominated performance in *Sarafina! Made in America; Sister Act; Sister Act 2: Back in the Habit; Ghosts of Mississippi,* and *Corrina, Corrina!* She has also appeared on a variety of television dramatic series, sitcoms, and specials, including HBO's now-historic "Comic Relief" series benefitting for the nation's homeless. It is co-hosted by Robin Williams and Billy Crystal.

Goldberg is well known for her tireless humanitarian efforts on behalf of children, the homeless, human rights, substance abuse, and the battle against AIDS, as well as many other worthwhile causes and charities. She has won countless awards and honors. In February 1995, prints of her hands, feet, and braids were immortalized in cement at Mann's Chinese Theater.

Whoopi continues to be in demand, starring in *Ghosts of Mississippi, Eddie,* and *How Stella Got Her Groove Back.* She is a frequent visitor on Hollywood Squares. She tells all in her autobiography *Whoopi!* She is a proud mother of one child.

161

HONORABLE MENTION

Science, Technology, and Health

James West M.D.
Vivian Penn M.D.
LaSalle Leffall M.D.
Louis Sullivan M.D.
Harold Freeman M.D.
Herbert Nickens M.D.
Reed Tucson M.D.
Isaiah Warner Engineer
Cynthia Adams Engineer
Dr. Mark Dean Engineer
Dr. Warren Miller Engineer
Marshall Jones, Engineer
James Winfield Mitchell, Engineer

Business

J. Bruce Llewellyn
Dave Bing
John Rogers
Herman Russell
Russell Simmons
Ed Gardner
Roy Roberts
Sylvia Rhone

Community Activism, Politics, Government, and Law

Congressman John Conyers
Rev. Al Sharpton
Julian Bond
Kwesi Mfume
Randall Robinson
Congressman J.C. Watts
Khalid Muhammad
A. Leon Higginbotham

Athletics

Warren Moon
Jerry Rice
Deion Sanders
Reggie White
Barry Sanders
Walter Payton
Bill Russell
Cynthia Cooper
Lenny Wilkens
Ricky Henderson
Bob Gibson
Michael Johnson
Marion Jones

Artists

Cynthia St. James
Tom Feelings
Romare Bearden
Annie Lee
Vannetta Honeywood
Charles Bibb

Literature and Media

Walter Mosley
E. Lynn Harris
Sonia Sanchez
Cathy Hughes
Tony Brown
Les Brown
Bob Law
Tom Joyner

Religion

Creflo Dollar
Wilton Gregory
John Kinney
John Bryant
Juanita Bynum
Vashti McKenzie

Education

Wade Nobles
Adelaide Sanford
Silas Purnell
Cornel West
Henry Louis Gates
Anyim Palmer

Entertainment

Sarah Vaughn
Richard Pryor
Marvin Gaye
Sam Cooke
Puff Daddy
Tupac
Kirk Franklin
Danny Glover
Alfre Woodard
Lauryn Hill
Robert Kelly
artist formerly known as Prince

NOTES

NOTES

NOTES

NOTES

NOTES

NOTES